George Eliot
Silas Marner: The Weaver of Raveloe

The George Eliot Fellowship of Japan

Edited with an Introduction, Notes, and Exercises
by
Hiroshi Ikezono
Fumiko Nishiyama
Chiyo Fujiwara

Osaka Kyoiku Tosho

はじめに

　この教科書は日本ジョージ・エリオット協会の設立20周年記念事業の企画を受けて作成したものです。その内容はエリオットの代表的作品を大学用英語教材として出版するというもので、本書はその第一弾となります。エリオットは英国を代表する小説家で、本国には歴史ある The George Eliot Fellowship という研究・愛好団体があります。日本ジョージ・エリオット協会（The George Eliot Fellowship of Japan）は1997年に設立され、この偉大な作家の研究や普及に大きな役割を果たしてきました。今回の企画の主旨は、エリオット作品の原文を教室で実際に読んで、その素晴らしさや魅力を味わっていただこうというものです。

　昨今、文学作品を教科書として編む場合、大学の英語教育を取り巻く厳しい状況に直面します。コミュニケーションの手段としての実用的な英語を学ぶ教材が多く求められ、文学作品を用いた教科書は減少しつつあります。もちろん、前者の必要性は否定すべくもありません。しかしながら、文学作品を通した英語力や異文化理解の涵養のプロセス——文学作品が持つ多彩な言語表現を読み解き、人間の言動や心情の機微を感受性豊かに理解し、さらには作品に具現化された作家の思想に触れながら、深いレベルでの異文化体験をする、等々——には、時代を問わず普遍的な意義と価値があります。そしてエリオットの小説はそのいずれの学びにも十分に応えうる豊かな資質を備えています。

　文学作品をより深く理解するためには、作家の伝記や思想的背景の紹介が有用であろうとの考えから、これらについて解説した Introduction を本書の冒頭に付しています。ですが、やや詳しい専門的な内容も含まれていますので、必ずしも最初に Introduction の項をすべて読んで網羅的に理解しておく必要はありません。まずは作品世界を楽しむことが大事ですので、本書の使い方の項をご一読の上、Unit 1 から始まる物語の内容に実際に触れてみてください。Introduction については、作品を読みつつ必要に応じて適宜参照するという用い方をされても結構です。本書を読んでさらにエリオットに関心を持った方には、この解説が将来の発展的学習の一助となることを期待します。

　本教科書の作成に際しては、企画母体である日本ジョージ・エリオット協会から諸方面にわたって心強い支援をいただきました。英文校正に関しては、山口大学の Ariel Keith Sorensen 氏と Nathaniel Tyler Edwards 氏にお手伝い願いました。さらに、横山哲彌氏をはじめとする大阪教育図書の方々には、本書の刊行にご尽力いただきました。この場をお借りして、すべての方々に厚く御礼申し上げます。

2017年12月

CONTENTS

はじめに …………………………………………………………………… 1
Introduction
 ジョージ・エリオットの生涯 ………………………………………… 3
 『サイラス・マーナー』の背景とジョージ・エリオットの思想 …… 6
本書の使い方 ……………………………………………………………… 12
主要登場人物 ……………………………………………………………… 14
Unit 1 Raveloe における Silas の暮らし ………………………… 16
Unit 2 Lantern Yard における事件 ……………………………… 22
Unit 3 Silas が執心する機(はた)と金 ………………………………… 28
Unit 4 Cass 家の兄弟 Godfrey と Dunsey …………………… 34
Unit 5 予期せぬ事件と Silas の心理 …………………………… 42
Unit 6 Godfrey と父 Squire Cass の葛藤 ……………………… 48
Unit 7 村の女性 Dolly と Nancy ………………………………… 54
Unit 8 幼子(おさなご)の出現 ………………………………………………… 60
Unit 9 Eppie がもたらすもの …………………………………… 66
Unit 10 16 年後 ……………………………………………………… 72
Unit 11 Godfrey と Nancy の葛藤 ……………………………… 78
Unit 12 Silas と Eppie の絆 ……………………………………… 84
Unit 13 それぞれの行く末 ………………………………………… 90
Unit 14 レポートを書こう ………………………………………… 96
  付録 ………………………………………………………………… 101

Introduction

ジョージ・エリオットの生涯

　『サイラス・マーナー』(*Silas Marner*) の作者ジョージ・エリオット (George Eliot) は、英国19世紀ヴィクトリア朝を代表する小説家の一人である。ジョージ・エリオットというのはペンネームで、本名はメアリ・アン・エヴァンズ (Mary Anne（後に Ann）Evans) という。1819年11月22日、英国イングランド中部にあるウォリックシャ地方で、父ロバート (Robert) と母クリスティアーナ (Christiana) の間に生まれた。二人の間には、メアリ・アンの他に、彼女とは5歳違いの姉クリスティアーナ (Christiana) と3歳違いの兄アイザック (Isaac) がいる。父は土地の名士ニューディゲイト (Newdigate) 家の広大な地所の土地差配人を務めた有能な人物で、メアリ・アンは子供の頃から彼のことをとても慕っていた。メアリ・アンは他者との愛情を強く求める性質だったことが知られている。彼女

ジョージ・エリオット
出典：ウィキメディア・コモンズ（Wikimedia Commons）

にとって父と同じくとりわけ愛情の対象だったのは兄アイザックで、彼らとの交流の様子は自伝的長編小説『フロス河の水車場』(*The Mill on the Floss*) に色濃く投影されている。

　多感な幼少時代の後、彼女は5歳で姉と同じ寄宿学校、9歳で別の寄宿学校に入っている。二つ目の学校で出会った教師マライア・ルイス (Maria Lewis, 1800?-87) は熱烈な福音主義者で、メアリ・アンは多大な感化を受けた。その覚醒した篤く禁欲的なキリスト教への信仰心は、学校を出た後もずっと変わらぬほどであった。一方、読書や語学に対する好奇心や探求心もまた、この時期に強く育まれた。数年後には別の学校に移るが、これらの学校時代、彼女は学業面での優秀さを発揮したという。

グリフ・ハウス

　その後メアリ・アンは自宅グリフ・ハウス (Griff House) に戻るが、1836年、16歳の時に母が病気のため死亡、翌年に姉が結婚、その4年後に兄が結婚というように家庭内の多くの変化を経験する。その間にも旺盛な読書欲は増し、その対象は文学のみならず哲学や自然科学など広範囲な分野に及んだ。また、イタリア語やドイツ語などの個人教授も受けている。彼女は愛する父の世話に従事することとなったが、1841年、父とともにグリフ・ハウスから近郊の町コヴェントリーの新たな住居へと引っ越した。ここで彼女の人生における一大転機が訪れる。

　それは、コヴェントリーで知り合った当時の自由思想家たち (free thinkers) との交流に端を発した、キリスト教の放棄という未知の経験であった。中でも急進的なチャールズ・ブレイ (Charles Bray, 1811-84) の教えや、その妻の兄チャールズ・ヘネル (Charles Hennell, 1809-50) の著書『キリスト教の起源に

関する研究』(An Inquiry concerning the Origin of Christianity, 1838) などの影響は大きかった。従来の宗教観を覆す彼らの先鋭的な思想はメアリ・アンを捉え、彼女はあれほど熱心に傾倒していたキリスト教の信仰を失うこととなった。この影響は家庭内にも及び、1842年1月、22歳の彼女は教会行きを拒んで父と争う事態にまで発展した。父への配慮から5月に教会行きは復活するものの、ブレイ家の人々との親交は続き、その延長上で1846年にドイツの神学者・哲学者ダーフィト・フリードリヒ・シュトラウス (David Friedrich Strauss, 1808-74) 著『イエスの生涯』(Das Leben Jesu, 1835-36)(英訳名 The Life of Jesus) を翻訳出版する。これら一連の流れに通底するのは、当時流布していた聖書の高等批評 (higher criticism) の姿勢である。これは、聖書を神による啓示の書とする従来の考えを捨て、人間の創造物として合理的、科学的、実証的に解釈し直すものであった。シュトラウスの著作はメアリ・アンの懐疑思想の深化に大きく寄与するものとなった。キリスト教関連の彼女の翻訳としては、他に1854年に出したドイツの哲学者ルートヴィヒ・アンドレアス・フォイエルバッハ (Ludwig Andreas Feuerbach, 1804-72) 著『キリスト教の本質』(Das Wesen des Christenthums, 1841)(英訳名 The Essence of Christianity) が有名だが、同じく多大な影響を与えることになった本書については後述する。

　1849年に父が亡くなった後、メアリ・アンの知的活動ならびに当時の知識層に接する機会はさらに拡大する。ロンドンへ出た彼女は、1851年に『ウェストミンスター・レヴュー』(The Westminster Review) という急進的な批評誌の副編集長に就任するまでになった。これより以前に、彼女は自身のことを Marian と称するようになっていた。メアリアンは精力的に活躍したが、一方で、『ウェストミンスター・レヴュー』への参加を促した主幹のジョン・チャップマン (John Chapman, 1821-94) との近しい関係が妻らに疑われるといった私生活上の問題も起きた。さらに、この雑誌を通して知己となった哲学者・社会学者のハーバート・スペンサー (Herbert Spencer, 1820-1903) に対し、彼女が叶わぬ恋愛感情を抱いたという出来事もあった。さらに、別の男性ジョージ・ヘンリー・ルイス (George Henry Lewes, 1817-78) との出会いは、その後の彼女の人生に最大の影響を与えることになる。

　ルイスの功績はメアリアンのパートナーとして生涯を共にした点にある。この場合のパートナーとは、愛情面のみならず、彼女を小説家として世に送り出すという文芸面での重要な役割を果たす存在だったことを意味している。二人が知り合った1851年当時、ルイスは既婚者で扶養家族があったが、夫婦関係は破綻状態にあった。当時の法律により離婚は不可能だったため、その数年後、ルイスとメアリアンは実質的な同棲生活に踏み切ることとなった。道徳観念の厳しかったヴィクトリア朝社会にあって、この決断はかなりの現実的かつ心理的困難を伴っていたことは想像に難くない。二人の関係はルイスが死去するまで続くこととなる。

　ルイスは様々な知的活動に従事していたが、文芸評論家でもあった彼はメアリアンに内在する文才を見出し、小説を書くことを熱心に勧めた。1856年9月、36歳の時に、彼女は最初の短編「エイモス・バートン師の悲運」("The Sad Fortunes of the Reverend Amos Barton") を書き始めた。翌年この作品は『ブラックウッズ・エディンバラ・マガジン』(Blackwood's Edinburgh Magazine) に公表され、1858年にはその他2編を集めた単行本『牧師たちの物語』(Scenes of Clerical Life) が出版された。注目したいのは、最初の短編に関して出版者ジョン・ブラックウッド (John Blackwood) へ送った書簡の中で、初めてジョージ・エリオットという名前が用いられた事実である。この短編は匿名で出されたものの、ほどなくして彼女のペンネームは読者の目に触れるこ

ジョージ・ヘンリー・ルイス
出典：ウィキメディア・コモンズ
(Wikimedia Commons)

とになった。男性ペンネーム使用の背景には、世に憚られる自身の同棲生活への配慮や、周囲からの評価に敏感で臆病なその性格、さらには、同時期の 1856 年 10 月に出した評論「女流作家の愚劣な小説」("Silly Novels by Lady Novelists") で批判したような芸術性の低い当時の女性作家の現状など、様々な要因があったことだろう。ジョージはルイスのファースト・ネームから、エリオットは発音の良さから採用されたのだという。

『牧師たちの物語』は好評を博し、翌年に初の長編『アダム・ビード』(Adam Bede) が出版されると、エリオットは各方面から称賛を受け、その地位を確立した。作家としては遅咲きの花ながら、その後の活躍はコンスタントであり、およそ 1 年から数年の間隔で、詩作品も含めた新作を世に出している。彼女が執筆した諸作品の中で、主要な小説は以下の通りである。

『牧師たちの物語』(*Scenes of Clerical Life*, 1858)
 三つの短編「エイモス・バートン師の悲運」("The Sad Fortunes of the Reverend Amos Barton")、「ギルフィル師の恋」("Mr Gilfil's Love-Story")、「ジャネットの悔悟」("Janet's Repentance") からなる。表題の通り、いずれの物語にも中心人物として牧師が登場し、彼らを巡る人生の諸相が描かれる。

『アダム・ビード』(*Adam Bede*, 1859)
 最初の長編。主人公アダム・ビードは美貌の娘に恋するが、彼女は裕福な地主の息子に熱を上げ、誘惑された末に捨てられる。最後には殺人罪を巡る裁判にまで発展するこの三角関係の顛末を中心として、各人物の苦悩や葛藤の様子が描かれる。

『フロス河の水車場』(*The Mill on the Floss*, 1860)
 作者の自伝的要素の濃い作品。主人公マギー・タリヴァー (Maggie Tulliver) は作者を彷彿とさせる。少女期における周囲の世界との交流、その後の家族の没落、青年期における報われぬ恋愛とその行く末が、表題のフロス河を中心的背景として描かれる。

『サイラス・マーナー』(*Silas Marner*, 1861)
 本書

『ロモラ』(*Romola*, 1863)
 15 世紀末イタリアのフィレンツェを舞台にした歴史小説で、実在の人物も多く登場する。主人公ロモラは野心家の男と結婚するが、後に夫は身を滅ぼす。彼女はいったんは偉大な宗教的指導者に師事するものの、やがて自らの進む道を見出していく。

『急進主義者フィーリクス・ホルト』(*Felix Holt, the Radical*, 1866)
 1832 年の第一次選挙法改正を背景にした政治的色彩の濃い作品。主人公フィーリクス・ホルトが時代の変革を試みる中で自分を支えてくれた女性と結ばれる物語と、政敵である旧家の息子、およびその母親の過去を巡る物語とが並行して描かれる。

『ミドルマーチ』(*Middlemarch*, 1871–72)
 表題の地方都市を舞台とし、境遇の異なる複数組の男女の人生を描く壮大なスケールの作品。中心をなすのは、それぞれに高邁な理想を抱きつつも挫折を経験する主人公ドロシア・ブルック (Dorothea Brooke) とターシアス・リドゲイト (Tertius Lydgate) の苦悩に満ちた人生の歩みである。

『ダニエル・デロンダ』(*Daniel Deronda*, 1876)
 最後の長編。英国育ちだがユダヤ人の血を引くことが判明した主人公ダニエル・デロンダがユダヤ民族解放運動に身を投じていく物語と、気位が高く尊大な女性グウェンドレン・ハーレス (Gwendolen Harleth) が不幸な結婚生活に陥っていく物語からなる。

1878年11月、エリオットが59歳の時に、彼女が長年にわたって苦楽を共にしたルイスが亡くなった。しばらく大きな悲嘆に暮れていた彼女だったが、翌年の春先にようやく知人らとの面会を再開する。その中の一人が、かねてよりエリオットとルイスに助力してくれていた青年実業家ジョン・ウォルター・クロス (John Walter Cross, 1840-1924) だった。その後クロスから求婚を受けた彼女は、翌1880年5月、60歳でこの20歳年下の男性と結婚する。ほどなくして、長年ルイスとの同棲生活を認めず疎遠になっていた兄アイザックからも祝福の便りが届いた。

　しかしエリオットの余生は短く、結婚からわずか7か月後の1880年12月22日、腎臓病により61歳の生涯を閉じた。当初はロンドンのウェストミンスター寺院への埋葬も検討されたが、キリスト教の放棄やルイスとの同棲生活など生前の経緯からこれは

エリオットの墓

見送られた。クロスの発案により、その亡骸はロンドン北部のハイゲート墓地に眠るルイスのそばに埋葬された。そして没後100年目に当たる1980年、ウェストミンスター寺院の「詩人記念隅」(Poets' Corner) にエリオットの名前が刻まれることになった。大教会堂に設けられたこの一画は、英国歴代の偉大な文人たちの墓や記念碑が所狭しと並べられており、文壇に顕著な功績を残したエリオットにふさわしい場所である。

『サイラス・マーナー』の背景とジョージ・エリオットの思想

　『サイラス・マーナー』はエリオットの三つ目の長編で、彼女の小説の中では比較的短く親しみやすい作品である。従来、エリオットの小説群は、自身が幼少期より馴染みのあった英国の伝統的田園社会を舞台とする情感豊かな前期作品と、深化した思想や倫理性が盛り込まれた知的で重厚な後期作品とに分類されることが多い。これに従えば、彼女自身が "a story of old-fashioned village life" (Haight, *Letters* 3: 371) と呼ぶ本小説は、前期の最後の作品に当たる。このことは同時に、この小説がエリオットの作家経歴における転換期に書かれた注目すべき作品であることも意味している。時系列的に見ると、次作『ロモラ』の構想や資料収集がすでに先行していたところへ、本人曰く "a sudden inspiration" (Haight, *Letters* 3: 371) により『サイラス・マーナー』の物語が割り込んできて、そちらを先に執筆することになったという。このことは本作品の位置づけを考える上で興味深い経緯である。

　『サイラス・マーナー』は出版当時から評判が良く、その後もたとえば "the most flawless of George Eliot's works" (138) というジョーン・ベネット (Joan Bennett) の言葉や、"*Silas Marner* is as perfect a work of prose fiction as any in the language, a small miracle" (118) というウォルター・アレン (Walter Allen) の言葉に表れているように、その完成度について批評家たちから高い評価を受けてきた。一方、エリオットを英国小説の「偉大な伝統」に属する一人として賞賛し、20世紀半ばにおける彼女の再評価に大きく貢献したF・R・リーヴィス (F. R. Leavis) は、本作品に関しては "something of the fairy-tale" (46) と捉えていて、扱いが小さい。この指摘自体は決して間違いとは言いきれないが、これに関連して言えば、以下のように、エリオットはそのおとぎ話的な要素を認識しつつも、さらに言葉を加えている。

> It came to me first of all, quite suddenly, as a sort of legendary tale, suggested by my recollection of having once, in early childhood, seen a linen-weaver with a bag on his back; but, as my mind dwelt on the subject, I became inclined to a more realistic treatment. (Haight, *Letters* 3: 382)

エリオットの言う「より写実的な書き方_{リアリスティック}」が具体的に作品のどの点に見られるかについてはいろいろな考え方があるだろう。小説全体として見れば、観察眼豊かな写実的要素と想像力豊かなおとぎ話的要素が見事に融合している点が、この作品の大きな魅力となっているのは間違いない。こうした写実性と想像性の融合はエリオット諸作品の特徴でもある。

　写実主義（realism）は 19 世紀ヴィクトリア朝小説の主潮をなした手法だが、エリオットはその第一人者であり、そのリアリズム信奉は初期の作品から表明されている。とりわけ有名なのは、長編第一作『アダム・ビード』第 17 章におけるリアリズム宣言である。

> So I am content to tell my simple story, without trying to make things seem better than they were; dreading nothing, indeed, but falsity, which, in spite of one's best efforts, there is reason to dread. Falsehood is so easy, truth so difficult. (222; ch.17)

虚偽を恐れ、あるがままの真実を描こうとするこの姿勢には、精緻な観察によって人生の複雑な諸相や実態を把握しようとする小説家エリオットの強い信念が窺える。これに続けて彼女は、同じように平凡な人間の真実の姿を描き出した 17 世紀オランダ絵画を称揚している。絵画の手法と文学の手法のつながりについては、小説作品以外にも言及がある。たとえば、小説家としてデビューする前年の 1856 年 4 月に『ウェストミンスター・レヴュー』に寄せた書評では、美術・社会評論家ジョン・ラスキン (John Ruskin, 1819-1900) の著書『近代画家論』(*Modern Painters*, 1843-60) 第 3 巻で主張された彼のリアリズム論に賛同し、"The truth of infinite value that he teaches is *realism*" (Haight, *Biography* 183) と述べている。また、同誌に掲載された評論でリアリズムへの強い意識が窺えるものとしては、同年 7 月の「ドイツ民族の自然史」("The Natural History of German Life") が挙げられる。ここでエリオットは、ドイツ農民の粗野で卑俗な実態を忠実に観察、記述した社会学者・民族学者ヴィルヘルム・ハインリヒ・リール (Wilhelm Heinrich Riehl, 1823-97) に共感し、"All the more sacred is the task of the artist when he undertakes to paint the life of the People. Falsification here is far more pernicious than in the more artificial aspects of life" (Pinney 271) と言明している。

　リアリズムが諸事象を美化せずあるがままに描き出すからには、結果として人間の持つ醜悪な暗い側面にまで光が当てられ、それが赤裸々に提示されることになるのは必然である。洞察力に長けたエリオットのリアリズムは、人間の内面心理においても迫真性 (verisimilitude) を追究する。このため、彼女の生み出す登場人物は、多くが深刻な心理的葛藤や挫折を経験する。この醜悪さの根底にある要因をあえて一つ挙げるなら、それは人間に内在するエゴイズム（egoism）ということになる。エリオット作品においては、このエゴイズムの主題が大きくクローズアップされることが多い。人間は誰しも自我 (ego, self) を持つが、一見ニュートラルな意味合いを持つこれらの名詞が形容詞化すると (egoistic, selfish)、否定的な意味合いを帯びるという事実は一考に値するだろう。そして、異なる自我を持つ個人の集合体が共同体社会ということになる。

　近代市民社会における人間は、それ以前の時代とは異なり、社会的な存在_{ソーシャル・ビーイング}に変化したとよく言われる。そこには 18 世紀産業革命に端を発する商工中産階級の台頭など、諸々の要因が関わっているだろう。英文学に絡めて言うと、この変化は 18 世紀以降に小説という文学の一形態が大きく開花していった現象と無縁ではない。庶民の識字率が向上していった近代以降、市井の人々が手に取り始めた

小説は、たとえば特定の英雄や神話を扱う壮大な叙事詩（古くは古期英語 (Old English) 時代の『ベーオウルフ』(*Beowulf*)、ルネサンス以降ではエドマンド・スペンサー (Edmund Spenser, 1552?-99) の『妖精の女王』(*The Faerie Queene*, 1590-96) やジョン・ミルトン (John Milton, 1608-74) の『失楽園』(*Paradise Lost*, 1667) などあまたある）とは異なり、卑近な個人と周囲の人間たち、つまり外部社会との関係を描くパターンが多い。19世紀の英国小説が18世紀のそれの延長上にあり、さらに進化発展を遂げたものであることは言うまでもない。エリオットは『急進主義者フィーリクス・ホルト』の中で、"there is no private life which has not been determined by a wider public life" (50; ch.3) と述べているが、これは彼女が個人と社会の相関関係、両者の相克や軋轢の諸相に対して強い関心と洞察を示していたことを表す一節である。

　エリオットが社会に言及する際、あるいは彼女の描く社会が論ぜられる際、「有機的」（organic）や「有機体」(organism) という語が用いられることが多い。たとえば、先に紹介した評論「ドイツ民族の自然史」において、エリオットは "the organic structure of society" (Pinney 293)、"the organic constitution of society" (Pinney 295) といった表現を使用し、またリールからの引用句 "the social organism" (Pinney 296) を提示しつつ、彼の業績を解説している。彼女の社会観に影響を与えたとされるのは、リールの社会学の他にも、フランスの哲学者・社会学者オーギュスト・コント (Auguste Comte, 1798-1857) や前述のハーバート・スペンサーらが唱えた「社会有機体論」(theory of social organism) の考え方がある。これは「社会を生物有機体のアナロジーで捉える社会観の総称」（廣松 698）で、社会の構成員は諸機能を持つ有機体の一部として社会全体の中で捉えられる。エリオットの知人だったスペンサーは、19世紀半ばに博物学者チャールズ・ダーウィン (Charles Darwin, 1809-82) らが提唱した生物進化論を社会的関係に適用する社会進化論を唱えた。また、パートナーのルイスは生物科学や心理学などの分野でも積極的に持論を世に発信し、彼女に知的刺激と影響を与えていた。このように当時の最先端の思想を取り込みながら、エリオットは個人と共同体社会の有機的関係について模索し、それを作品に具現化していったのである。

　ここでエゴイズムに話を戻そう。エリオットは後期の大作『ミドルマーチ』において、"We are all of us born in moral stupidity, taking the world as an udder to feed our supreme selves" (211; ch.21) と記している。人間は皆「道徳的愚鈍」に生まれていて、周囲の世界を自分たちの「至高の自我」を養う乳房だと捉えているという認識には、エゴイズムに対するエリオットの考えが端的に集約されている。道徳という概念もエリオットを語る上では欠かせない。エリオットは道徳性への意識が高い作家であるという評価は広く確立されている。道徳というといかにもしかつめらしいイメージを伴うが、実際、さながらメンターのごとき作者の主張が作品中で前面に現れることが少なくない。しかし、これは裏を返せば人生に対する彼女の真摯でひたむきな姿勢の証左に外ならない。いわゆる芸術至上主義は「芸術のための芸術」(art for art's sake) を標榜するが、エリオットの場合は、その反意表現である「人生のための芸術」(art for life's sake) を体現する作家と言えるのではなかろうか。このあたりは、文学の目的は "a criticism of life" (228) にあると主張した同時代の詩人・批評家マシュー・アーノルド (Matthew Arnold, 1822-88) と通ずるものがある。芸術と人生の調和的融合はエリオットの目標とするところであった。人間の不可避的エゴイズムへの認識は、この延長上に捉えることができるのであり、決して厭世的なものではない。これらのことは、"Art is the nearest thing to life; it is a mode of amplifying experience and extending our contact with our fellow-men beyond the bounds of our personal lot" (Pinney 271) という彼女の言葉に顕著に表れている。人間は各々エゴイズムを内包するからこそ、その狭量な枠を超越した外界の同胞とのつながりが重要なのであり、その拡張にこそ芸術の存在意義があるのだ。

そのようなエリオットにとって、自身の芸術が目的とするところは、人間同士の「共感」(sympathy) の拡大にある。彼女は随所でこの言葉を用いているが、よく引き合いに出される代表的なものをいくつか列記してみよう。

> The greatest benefit we owe to the artist, whether painter, poet, or novelist, is the extension of our sympathies. (Pinney 270)

> My own experience and development deepen every day my conviction that our moral progress may be measured by the degree in which we sympathize with individual suffering and individual joy. (Haight, *Letters* 2: 403)

> If Art does not enlarge men's sympathies, it does nothing morally. (Haight, *Letters* 3: 111)

二つ目と三つ目の例からは、エリオットにとって共感と道徳の概念が密接に結びついている事実も窺い知れるだろう。さらに重要なのは、こうした人間同士の共感に対する主張が、単なる情緒的あるいは教訓的な発想から生じているのではなく、彼女の宗教観の変遷と深く関連している点である。

「ジョージ・エリオットの生涯」で紹介したように、エリオットは当時の先進的自由主義思想に触れてキリスト教信仰を失うに至った。その後、それに代わる精神的礎を彼女に与えることになったものの一つに、1854年に翻訳出版したドイツの哲学者フォイエルバッハ著『キリスト教の本質』の思想がある。これは従来のキリスト教解釈を否定する書で、フォイエルバッハは、神の概念は人間の理想や願望を投影した想像的創造物であり、神の本質は実のところ人間の本質に他ならない、すなわち「神が人間であり、人間が神である」(27) と主張した。「もし、神が愛であるが、しかしこの愛の本質的な内容が人間であるならば、そのときは神的存在者（本質）の内容が人間的本質なのではないか？人間に対する神の愛は宗教の根底であり中心点である。しかし、人間に対する神の愛は、人間自身に対する人間の愛が、最高の真理・人間の最高の本質として対象化され直観されたものではないか？」(148) と説く彼の人間主義的、人間学的思想の影響は大きかった。また、フォイエルバッハは「愛は共同感情（ミット・ゲフュール）を離れては考えられず、また共同苦悩（ミット・ライデン）を離れては考えられない」(141) と述べたが、「共同感情」(Mitgefühl) や「共同苦悩」(Mitleiden) という概念がエリオットの「共感」と通ずることは明らかであろう。彼女は小説家に転身する前年、福音主義の偏狭な教義（ドグマ）を批判した評論「福音主義の教え —— カミング博士」("Evangelical Teaching: Dr. Cumming") において、"The idea of a God . . . is an extension and multiplication of the effects produced by human sympathy" (Pinney 188) というように、神の概念と人間の共感の関係性について言及している。また、1874年に書かれた書簡の一節 "the idea of God, so far as it has been a high spiritual influence, is the ideal of a goodness entirely human (i.e., an exaltation of the human)" (Haight, *Letters* 6: 98) は、最後の小説『ダニエル・デロンダ』の構想段階にあっても、彼女の信念は変わらなかったことを示している。

このようなエリオットの宗教観は "religion of humanity" と総称されることが多い。「人間教」「人類教」「人道教」「人間性の宗教」などと様々に翻訳されるこの言葉は、もともとはコントが提唱した考えで、彼女にとってはフォイエルバッハの思想と基調を同じくするものと考えられた。コントは「人類を真の究極的な実在と認め、「愛を原理に、秩序を基礎とし、進歩を目的とする」協調と連帯のとれた人類社会を形成するために、万人は自欲を制して愛他精神に徹し、至高の存在である人類を神と崇めていっさいの行動をそのために傾注すべきであると説き」(森岡 805)、これを "religion de l'humanité" と称した。ルイスが1840年代にコントと直接知り合っていたこともあり、エリオットは彼の実証主義的著作を数多く読んでいたが、上記のような思想は彼女の考えと通じるものがある。コントの説く「愛

他精神」すなわち利他主義 (altruism) が、人間に内在する「自欲」すなわち利己主義 (egoism) を超越した同胞愛や共感を尊ぶエリオットの考えに共鳴するのは言うまでもない。

　エリオットを19世紀という時代を要約する最大の文人であると述べた批評家バジル・ウィリー (Basil Willey) は、その精神的軌跡について、"Starting from evangelical Christianity, the curve passes through doubt to a reinterpreted Christ and a religion of humanity" (205) と的確に総括している。これは、程度や種類の差はあれ、19世紀ヴィクトリア朝の知識人たちが辿った軌跡とも重なっていた。同時に、"She was not, of course, a 'practising Christian', but in her estrangement from the 'religion *about* Jesus' she was none the further from the 'religion *of* Jesus'" (238) という彼の指摘もまた妥当なものであろう。エリオットは伝統的なキリスト教の教義自体からは袂を分かったものの、その底に流れる宗教的精神、すなわち人道主義的な根本姿勢は生涯保持し続けた。そのようなエリオットの人間観や人生観は決して揺らぐことなく彼女の諸作品に浸透している。エリオットのリアリズムは人間の醜悪さや脆弱さを顕在化させるが、その一方で、彼女の "religion of humanity" の精神は人間の存在意義や道徳的進歩への信頼を失うことなく、その集合体である有機的社会の可能性を模索し続けたのである。このことは、たとえば『ミドルマーチ』の最後を飾る有名な言葉によく表れているだろう。

> But the effect of her [Dorothea] being on those around her was incalculably diffusive: for the growing good of the world is partly dependent on unhistoric acts; and that things are not so ill with you and me as they might have been, is half owing to the number who lived faithfully a hidden life, and rest in unvisited tombs. (838; Finale)

物語の主人公ドロシアは確かに歴史に足跡を残すこともない卑小な存在である。だが、彼女のような人間の誠実な生き方は、周囲との関係性の中で波及的影響を及ぼし、それが社会の漸次的進展へと寄与するのだと結ぶこのくだりは、エリオットの思想が顕著に示された感動的な一節である。

　ここで『サイラス・マーナー』に話を戻すと、この作品においても、以上のようなエリオットの諸体験や思想の影響は随所に見出すことができる。これから本書を手にする読者のため詳述は避けるが、たとえばリアリズムに関しては、主要人物の一人ゴドフリー・カスの葛藤を巡るプロットにはそれがよく表れていると言えるだろう。人間のエゴイズムや社会との関係性は、主人公サイラス・マーナーはもちろんのこと、他の多くの登場人物に関わる命題である。また、この小説のところどころに描かれるキリスト教や宗教的意識は全体としてどのような意味を持つのか、エリオットの人道主義的姿勢は具体的にどのように反映されているのか、など考察の余地は多分にある。彼女は出版者ブラックウッドに宛てた書簡の中で、本作品について、"But I hope you will not find it at all a sad story, as a whole, since it sets—or is intended to set—in a strong light the remedial influences of pure, natural human relations. The Nemesis is a very mild one" (Haight, *Letters* 3: 382) と述べている。小説の展開に大いなる期待を抱かせる著者のこの言を念頭に置きつつ、この物語を楽しんでいただきたい。

　最後に付言すると、1900年から2年あまり英国へ留学した夏目漱石（金之助）は、帰国後の1903年に東京帝国大学で教鞭を執った際、『サイラス・マーナー』を授業で教えている。漱石はもちろん小説家として著名だが、同時に、英文学を専門とする英語教師としての顔を持っていた。漱石で教師と言えば『坊ちゃん』がすぐに思い起こされるだろうが、彼は優れた英文学者でもあり、大学での講義録をもとにした『文学論』(1907) と『文学評論』(1909) はその成果である。エリオットが逝去した23年後に、早くも『サイラス・マーナー』が日本で教えられていた事実には感慨深いものがある。明治時代の偉大な文豪と、

本教科書を手にする現代の読者とは、実は遠い縁(えにし)でつながっていると言えるのではなかろうか。

〈引用文献〉

Allen, Walter. *George Eliot*. New York: Macmillan, 1964.

Arnold, Matthew. *English Literature and Irish Politics*. Ed. R. H. Super. The Complete Prose Works of Matthew Arnold. Vol. 9. Ann Arbor: U of Michigan P, 1973.

Bennett, Joan. *George Eliot: Her Mind and Her Art*. Cambridge: Cambridge UP, 1948.

Eliot, George. *Adam Bede*. 1859. Harmondsworth: Penguin, 1988.

——. *Felix Holt, the Radical*. 1866. Harmondsworth: Penguin, 1995.

——. *Middlemarch*. 1871-72. Harmondsworth: Penguin, 1994.

Haight, Gordon S. *George Eliot: A Biography*. Oxford: Oxford UP, 1968. Harmondsworth: Penguin, 1985.

——, ed. *The George Eliot Letters*. 9 vols. New Haven: Yale UP, 1954-78.

Leavis, F. R. *The Great Tradition*. London: Chatto, 1948.

Pinney, Thomas, ed. *Essays of George Eliot*. London: Routledge, 1963.

Willey, Basil. *Nineteenth Century Studies: Coleridge to Matthew Arnold*. London: Chatto, 1949.

フォイエルバッハ『キリスト教の本質』上　船山信一訳　岩波書店, 1937.

廣松渉, 他編『岩波哲学・思想事典』岩波書店, 1998.

森岡清美, 他編『新社会学辞典』有斐閣, 1993.

本書の使い方

　『サイラス・マーナー』はエリオット作品の中では比較的短いとはいえ、原著で200ページ前後の長さがある。ゆえに、まずは原著から主要人物を巡る物語を中心に半期（半年）で読める分量の英文を選び、さらに、物語内容が理解できるように日本語のあらすじを補足的に加えることで、全体で一つの読み物として通読できるようにした。

全体の構成

　本書は全部で14のUnitにより構成されている。一回の授業につき1 Unitのペースで進むことを想定している。このうちUnit 13までは英文講読用で、各Unitには原著から抜粋した英文がPart 1・Part 2という形で二つ収録されている。Unit 14では、それまで読んできた内容を踏まえて、レポートの作成準備に取り組む。

注釈

　注釈はすぐに参照できるように右ページに置いた。種々の英英辞典からの記述を意識的に多く入れてあるが、これは注釈においても英語学習を促したいとの願いからである。もちろん、同時に英和辞書での意味確認を行うことも多いと思うが、そのような際にも、各語句がどのように英語で表現されるのかを吟味することには大きな意味がある。あるいは逆に、注釈の英英定義をもとに、それに相当する日本語表現を英和辞書で発見する作業もまた、英語学習に寄与するだろう。英和辞書のみでは得られない知見や楽しさに多く触れてもらいたい。

　なお、既出内容については「○ページ○行目を参照」というように相互参照ができるようにした。毎回すべての項目を振り返る必要はないかもしれないが、状況に応じて活用してもらいたい。

EXERCISES

　各Unitの最後に、各Partに関する課題を二種類ずつ置いた。一つ目は本文の内容把握を問う選択問題である。二つ目は、本文から重要だと思われるキーワードやキーフレーズを各自で自由に選び出し、その理由を考える課題である。エリオットの味わい深い英語と真摯に向き合う中で、感性やオリジナリティに富んだ多くの発見をしてもらいたい。加えて、この作業は最終的にはUnit 14のレポート作成に資することが期待される。

　二つのUnitごとに、物語内容を日本語で要約する課題をつけた。学習した複数の英文箇所に留意しつつ、限られた字数内でプロットの整理を行うには、それなりの力量を要する。英文を速読方式で読み返すことで、物語への理解がさらに深まるという効果も期待される。

コラム

　本書のところどころに各種コラムをつけた。内容は、コラムのあるUnitあるいはその周辺箇所に関する補足や、作品の読み方のヒントとなるようなコメントである。スペースの関係もあるが、あえて説明しすぎることのないよう簡潔な記述を心がけた。学習者の発展的学習を期待したい。コラムの中には、最後のレポート作成に役立つ素材があるかもしれない。EXERCISES中のキーワードやキーフレーズを選び出す課題と併せて利用してもらいたい。

本書および注釈に使用した書籍

　本書の作成に際しては Everyman's Library 版 (1993) を底本とした。ただし、教科書の全体的なスタイル統一のため、引用符については基本的にダブルの引用符 (" ") を、さらにその中に用いる引用符についてはシングルの引用符 (' ') を使用した。
　以下は注釈を施す際に使用した各種書籍の表記法である。

以下の原著の巻末注釈については、(　) 内のように記した。
　　Eliot, George. *Silas Marner: The Weaver of Raveloe*. 1861. Ed. David Carroll. Harmondsworth: Penguin, 1996. (Penguin 版注釈)
　　——. *Silas Marner: The Weaver of Raveloe*. 1861. Ed. Terence Cave. Oxford: Oxford UP, 1996. (Oxford 版注釈)
　　——. *Silas Marner: The Weaver of Raveloe*. 1861. Ed. Minoru Toyoda. Tokyo: Kenkyusha, 1929. (研究社版注釈)

以下の英英辞書については、(　) 内のような略称で記した。
　　The Oxford English Dictionary. 2nd ed. 2009. (*OED*)
　　The New Shorter Oxford English Dictionary. 4th ed. 1993. (*NSOED*)
　　Oxford Advanced Learner's Dictionary of Current English. 9th ed. 2015. (*OALD*)
　　Oxford Dictionary of English. 2nd ed. 2003. (*ODE*)
　　Longman Dictionary of Contemporary English. New ed. 1991. (*LDCE*)
　　Collins COBUILD Advanced Learner's English Dictionary. New digital ed. 2004. (*COBUILD*)

以下の英和辞書および百科事典については、書名をそのまま記した。
　　『研究社新英和大辞典』第 6 版 2006.
　　『リーダーズ英和辞典』第 2 版 2002.
　　『ジーニアス英和大辞典』第 1 版 2001-02.
　　『ブリタニカ国際大百科事典』電子辞書対応小項目版 2006.

以下の文法書については、書名をそのまま記した。
　　江川泰一郎『英文法解説』金子書房 , 1991.
　　綿貫陽 , 他『ロイヤル英文法』旺文社 , 2000.

方言に関する以下の書籍については、『方言研究』と略記した。
　　細江逸記『ヂョーヂ・エリオットの作品に用ひられたる英國中部地方言の研究』泰文堂 , 1935.

聖書については以下のものを使用し、本文中での記載は省略した。
　　英語版：Authorized Version (King James Version)
　　日本版：新共同訳 (日本聖書協会)

その他、使用回数が一回のみの書籍については、本文中に文献情報を記した。

主要登場人物

Silas Marner
主人公。Lantern Yard での事件をきっかけに Raveloe の村に移り住み、機織り職人として暮らす。人生においていくつかの予期せぬ出来事に遭遇し翻弄される。

William Dane
Lantern Yard における Silas の親友。

Sarah
Lantern Yard における Silas の婚約者。

Squire Cass
Raveloe の名高い地主(スクワイア)。息子たちへの心配や不満が絶えない。

Godfrey Cass
Squire Cass の長男で跡取り息子。持ち前の性格により、人生の困難を招く。

Dunstan (Dunsey) Cass
Squire Cass の次男で兄とは犬猿の仲。重大事件を引き起こし、姿を消す。

Nancy Lammeter
名家の娘で、後に Godfrey の妻となる。

Jem Rodney
もぐら捕りや密猟で生計を立てる村人。

Mr Macey
仕立て屋兼教区教会書記。

Dolly Winthrop
車大工の妻。親身になって Silas の世話する。

Aaron
Dolly の息子。

Mr Kimble
Godfrey の叔父で薬剤師。

Molly Farren
Godfrey の自堕落な妻。

Eppie
Godfrey と Molly の娘。幼少期に Silas と運命的な出会いをする。

George Eliot
Silas Marner: The Weaver of Raveloe

Unit 1　Raveloe における Silas の暮らし

原著第1章(1)

その昔、田舎の農家で糸車が用いられていた時代、よそからやってきた見慣れぬ機織り職人たちは、地元の住人からうさんくさい目で見られていた。当時、織物の商売は悪魔が関与しているという根拠のない迷信があった。古い時代の農夫たちは、自分たちの経験の及ばぬ外の世界を理解できず、素性の知れぬ行商人や移住してきたよそ者に不信の目を向けた。それらの人々が知識や手仕事に長けている場合はとりわけそうだった。機敏で器用な所作は魔術の性質を帯びているように考えられた。このようにして、田舎の土地に移り住んだ機織り職人たちは、死ぬまで隣人たちからよそ者と見なされ、また、そうした孤独につきものの偏屈な習慣が身についてしまうのが常だった。

Part 1

　In the early years of this century, such a linen-weaver, named Silas Marner, worked at his vocation in a stone cottage that stood among the nutty hedgerows near the village of Raveloe, and not far from the edge of a deserted stone-pit. The questionable sound of Silas's loom, so unlike the natural cheerful trotting of the
5　winnowing-machine, or the simpler rhythm of the flail, had a half-fearful fascination for the Raveloe boys, who would often leave off their nutting or birds'-nesting to peep in at the window of the stone cottage, counterbalancing a certain awe at the mysterious action of the loom, by a pleasant sense of scornful superiority, drawn from the mockery of its alternating noises, along with the bent, tread-mill attitude of
10　the weaver. But sometimes it happened that Marner, pausing to adjust an irregularity in his thread, became aware of the small scoundrels, and, though chary of his time, he liked their intrusion so ill that he would descend from his loom, and, opening the door, would fix on them a gaze that was always enough to make them take to their legs in terror. For how was it possible to believe that those large brown protuberant
15　eyes in Silas Marner's pale face really saw nothing very distinctly that was not close to them, and not rather that their dreadful stare could dart cramp, or rickets, or a wry mouth at any boy who happened to be in the rear? They had, perhaps, heard their fathers and mothers hint that Silas Marner could cure folks' rheumatism if he had a mind, and add, still more darkly, that if you could only speak the devil fair enough,
20　he might save you the cost of the doctor.

1 **this century** 19世紀。この小説が発表されたのは1861年で、語り手は同時代の読者に向かって語りかけている。
3 **stone-pit** = a pit from which stones are dug, a quarry (*OED*) 「石切場」 40ページの原著第4章あらすじも参照。
4 **loom** 「織機」 41ページの図版を参照。
5 **winnowing-machine** 「唐箕(とうみ)」箱形の胴につけた羽根車で起こした風を吹きつけて穀粒ともみ殻を分離する脱穀機。41ページの図版を参照。
5 **flail** 「殻竿(からざお)」刈り取った穀物に先端部分を打ちつけて脱穀する棒状の道具。41ページの図版を参照。
6 **leave off** = stop
6 **birds'-nesting** 「(ひなや卵をとるために) 鳥の巣を探すこと」
7 **counterbalancing** counterbalance A by B = 「BによってAと釣り合わせる、Aを相殺する、Aの埋め合わせをする」 e.g. The extra cost of mail order may be counterbalanced by its convenience.（通信販売の割増料金はその利便性によって埋め合わせられるかもしれない。）(*ODE*)
8 **a pleasant sense of scornful superiority** cf. a sense of superiority =「優越感」
8 **drawn from ...** 「…から得られた、…に基づいた」 e.g. There were two inferences to be drawn from her letter.（彼女の手紙から二つの推測が得られた。）(*COBUILD*) drawn from ... the weaver は直前の a pleasant sense of scornful superiority を修飾している句。
9 **alternating** alternate [ɔ́ːltərnèit] (vi.) = occur in turn repeatedly (*ODE*) cf. 名詞と形容詞の発音は[ɔ́ːltərnət]
9 **tread-mill** ここでは形容詞で「踏み車を踏んでいるような（姿勢）」の意。treadmill（踏み車）は囚人への刑罰の一つで、階段を上るような動きが単調に続き、囚人たちにとって大きな苦痛となった。41ページの図版を参照。
10 **it happened that ...** It happens that S+V =「たまたま…である、時に…ということが起こる」
11 **though chary of his time** = though (he was) chary (=sparing) of his time
12 **liked ... ill** like ill (arch.) = dislike (*OED*)
13 **take to their legs** take to one's legs [heels] = run away
14 **how was it possible to believe ...?** 「どうして信じることができただろうか」=「信じることはできなかった」 これを修辞疑問（rhetorical question）または反語という。
16 **not rather that ...** 14行目の how was it possible to believe と結びつく。つまり、how was it possible not to believe rather that ...? =「むしろ…を信じないということがどうしてできただろうか」=「むしろ…を信じることができた」
16 **dart ... at ~** 「~に対して…を放つ、投げつける」 ここでは、「cramp, rickets, a wry mouth などの病気を投げつけてくる」、つまり「病気にさせる」の意。
16 **cramp** 「痙攣、こむらがえり」
16 **rickets** 「佝僂病(くる)、骨軟化症」 複数形に見えるが rickets が原形。
16 **a wry mouth** 「口歪み」 顔面の歪みが直らない状態。 wry = twisted
19 **mind** = intention have a mind to do =「…したい気持ちがある」
19 **darkly** = in a threatening, mysterious, or ominous way (*ODE*) 「ひそかに、気味悪げに」
19 **speak the devil fair** fair = civilly, courteously, kindly この意味は speak (a person) fair という句でのみ用いられる。(*OED*) the devil は「やつ、あの厄介な男」の意で、ここではサイラス・マーナーを指している。また、あらすじにある通り、織物の商売には悪魔が関与しているという迷信があったので、文字通りの「悪魔」という意味も込められている。

Part 2

And Raveloe was a village where many of the old echoes lingered, undrowned by new voices. Not that it was one of those barren parishes lying on the outskirts of civilization—inhabited by meagre sheep and thinly-scattered shepherds: on the contrary, it lay in the rich central plain of what we are pleased to call Merry England, and held farms which, speaking from a spiritual point of view, paid highly-desirable tithes. But it was nestled in a snug well-wooded hollow, quite an hour's journey on horseback from any turnpike, where it was never reached by the vibrations of the coach-horn, or of public opinion. It was an important-looking village, with a fine old church and large churchyard in the heart of it, and two or three large brick-and-stone homesteads, with well-walled orchards and ornamental weathercocks, standing close upon the road, and lifting more imposing fronts than the rectory, which peeped from among the trees on the other side of the churchyard . . . .

It was fifteen years since Silas Marner had first come to Raveloe; he was then simply a pallid young man, with prominent, short-sighted brown eyes, whose appearance would have had nothing strange for people of average culture and experience, but for the villagers near whom he had come to settle it had mysterious peculiarities which corresponded with the exceptional nature of his occupation, and his advent from an unknown region called "North'ard". So had his way of life:—he invited no comer to step across his door-sill, and he never strolled into the village to drink a pint at the Rainbow, or to gossip at the wheelwright's: he sought no man or woman, save for the purposes of his calling, or in order to supply himself with necessaries; and it was soon clear to the Raveloe lasses that he would never urge one of them to accept him against her will—quite as if he had heard them declare that they would never marry a dead man come to life again.

コラム1: エリオット作品の時代設定

エリオットは小説作品のすべてにおいて時代を過去に設定している。とりわけ多いのは、執筆時点より一、二世代ほど前の過去である。Part 1 冒頭に書かれているように、本小説は19世紀初頭を舞台として始まる。他の作品を見てみると、彼女が最初に執筆した短編 "The Sad Fortunes of the Reverend Amos Barton" は、25年前の回想という体裁をとっている。長編第一作 Adam Bede では物語の始まりが1799年であることが明記されている。次作 The Mill on the Floss は具体的な年代が記されていないが、諸々の歴史的言及から、物語は1829年に始まると推定されている。後期作品の Felix Holt, the Radical と Middlemarch は、1832年の第一次選挙法改正法案 (The Reform Bill) の前後を時代背景としつつ、プロットが組み立てられているという共通点がある。これらに対し、最後の作品 Daniel Deronda になると、舞台は1864-66年で執筆時と比較的近い設定となっている。以上と大きく異なっているのは、15世紀末を舞台とする Romola であるが、この作品は当時のイタリアに関する史的調査に基づいて歴史小説を書くという特別な意図のもとに執筆されており、エリオット作品の中では例外的に捉えることができよう。

1 **the old echoes**「古い時代の残響、名残」「古い時代」とは 18 世紀半ばに起きた産業革命以前、あるいはその影響がまだ及んでいない時代を指す。2 行目の voices、7 行目の vibrations と併せて、音を連想させる語を作者が意図的に用いていると考えられる。
1 **undrowned**「聞こえなくなっていない、かき消されていない」 drown [dráun] は音を連想させる語と共に用いられることによって、「（より大きな音によって別の音を）聞こえなくする」という意味を持つ。
2 **new voices** 上記の the old echoes と対照的に用いられた表現で、産業革命の影響を受けて工業や文化が発展を遂げた 19 世紀の新たな気運を表している。
2 **Not that …**「（といっても）…というわけではない」It is not that … の省略形として成句化した表現。
2 **parishes**「教区」「教会区」 英国国教会の牧師が管轄する区域で、各々教会を保有していた。教区牧師は区民が納める十分の一税（6 行目の注を参照）などによって生計を立て、区民の精神生活を支えていた。
4 **the rich central plain**「ミッドランズ」(Midlands) と呼ばれるイングランド中部地方の実り豊かな平原のこと。作者の故郷であるウォリックシャ (Warwickshire) がモデルになっていると思われる。本書 Introduction を参照。
5 **held** hold = have enough space for; contain (*OALD*)
5 **spiritual** = religious, sacred 直後に登場する highly-desirable tithes の世俗性と対比させ、作者が意図的に用いた皮肉である。
6 **tithes** tithe [táið] =「十分の一税」 教会および牧師の生活の維持のために、教区民が 1 年間の収益の十分の一を穀物や家畜などで物納したもの。1836 年の「十分の一税金納化法」(Tithe Commutation Act) 制定後は金納することとなった。
7 **turnpike**「通行料取り立て門」「（有料の）街道」 41 ページの図版を参照。元来、公道の維持管理責任や費用負担は教区にあったが、交通量の増加に伴って民間運営団体に委託された。通行料を利用者に求めるこの新たな方式は、とりわけ 18 世紀後半から 19 世紀前半にかけて普及の拡大を見たが、料金徴収の不正など様々な弊害も生じたため、19 世紀半ば以降になると廃止の方向へ向かった。
9 **churchyard** = an area of land around a church, often used for burying people in (*OALD*) 直前の church との違いに留意。
9 **brick-and-stone homesteads**「煉瓦と石を用いて建てられた屋敷」
10 **close upon …** close [klóus] は副詞。upon = by the side of; along e.g. a hotel on the lake, Stratford-upon-Avon upon は on と同義でほとんど区別はないが、文語的である。
11 **lifting**「高く掲げて見せている、そびえ立たせている」 standing と同格で、意味上の主語は homesteads。
15 **would have had** 仮定法過去完了。If 節を用いて書き換えると、whose appearance would have had nothing strange if people of average culture and experience had seen it となる。
18 **North'ard** = Northward 「（ミッドランズから見て）北の方、北の地方」 29 ページのコラム 2 も参照。
18 **So had his way of life** 倒置構文。cf. "She was in London for years." "So was I."
20 **a pint** 液量の単位で約 0.57 リットル。酒場で注文する際「1 パイント」あるいは「半パイント」(half-pint) と言う。現在でも英国の酒場、パブ (pub=public house の略) で各種ビールを注文する時に用いられている。
20 **the Rainbow** 居酒屋兼宿屋の「虹亭」。村に住む者たちの社交場となっている。43 ページ下部のあらすじも参照。
21 **save** = except
21 **calling** = a profession or career (*OALD*)
23 **accept** = <dated> say yes to a proposal of marriage from (a man) (*ODE*)

Part 1 EXERCISES

A 以下の設問に答えなさい。

1. What information is given concerning Silas?
    a. He sometimes shows a kindly interest in the Raveloe boys' attention.
    b. He is so confident in his handicraft that he does not care about mistakes.
    c. He has no particular occupation other than linen-weaving.
    d. His eyesight is strong enough to make the Raveloe boys scared.

2. How do the Raveloe boys react to Silas?
    a. They are attracted by the sound of his winnowing-machine.
    b. They do not stop playing around in order to find out what he is doing in his cottage.
    c. They like to see him approaching them because they are superior.
    d. They think themselves better than him because of the strange noises and his bearing.

3. What is this passage mainly about?
    a. Silas's distant relationship with the Raveloe boys
    b. Silas's generous attitude towards the Raveloe boys
    c. Silas's superhuman attention to the Raveloe boys
    d. Silas's decreasing popularity among the Raveloe boys

B 原文の中であなたが重要だと思ったキーワードやキーフレーズを二つ選び、それらを書き出しなさい。また、それらを選んだ理由について、それぞれ日本語で簡潔に説明しなさい。

1. キーワードやキーフレーズ (　　　　) 行目

   理由

2. キーワードやキーフレーズ (　　　　) 行目

   理由

Part 2 EXERCISES

A 以下の設問に答えなさい。

1. What kind of place is Raveloe?
    a. It is a densely populated area.
    b. It can hardly enjoy the blessings of nature.
    c. It is significantly influenced by civilization.
    d. It still maintains ties with the past.

2. In line 4, the phrase "Merry England" is closest in meaning to _____.
    a. England that has urbanized town communities
    b. England that preserves what evokes nostalgia
    c. England that is adored by those living abroad
    d. England that is regarded as highly sophisticated

3. How is Silas in Raveloe described?
    a. His appearance is always remarkable, compared with average people.
    b. His "North'ard" origin helps the villagers appreciate his vocation.
    c. He tries to keep himself as apart from the villagers as possible.
    d. He avoids contact with the villagers even if it has something to do with weaving.

4. What does the word "it" in line 16 refer to?
    a. Raveloe   b. Silas's appearance   c. culture   d. experience

B 原文の中であなたが重要だと思ったキーワードやキーフレーズを二つ選び、それらを書き出しなさい。また、それらを選んだ理由について、それぞれ日本語で簡潔に説明しなさい。

1. キーワードやキーフレーズ (　　　　) 行目

   理由

2. キーワードやキーフレーズ (　　　　) 行目

   理由

Unit 2　Lantern Yard における事件

原著第 1 章 (2)

> サイラス・マーナーについて、ラヴィロウの村ではいろいろな憶測が流れた。ある晩、村人のジェム・ロドニー (Jem Rodney) は、発作により意識をなくして硬直したサイラスの姿を目撃した。これを聞いた村人たちは、彼の身体からは魂が出たり入ったりするのだと噂した。また、彼の持っている薬草に関する知識も不審がられた。しかし同時に、その機織り職人としての仕事ぶりは一定の評価を得ていた。こうして15年の歳月が流れた。彼に対する印象にそれほど変化は生じていなかったが、ただ一つ、サイラスがどこかに大金をためこんでいるという噂が付け加わっていた。

Part 1

　　But while opinion concerning him had remained nearly stationary, and his daily habits had presented scarcely any visible change, Marner's inward life had been a history and a metamorphosis, as that of every fervid nature must be when it has fled, or been condemned to solitude. His life, before he came to Raveloe, had been filled
5　with the movement, the mental activity, and the close fellowship, which, in that day as in this, marked the life of an artisan early incorporated in a narrow religious sect, where the poorest layman has the chance of distinguishing himself by gifts of speech, and has, at the very least, the weight of a silent voter in the government of his community. Marner was highly thought of in that little hidden world, known
10　to itself as the church assembling in Lantern Yard; he was believed to be a young man of exemplary life and ardent faith; and a peculiar interest had been centred in him ever since he had fallen, at a prayer-meeting, into a mysterious rigidity and suspension of consciousness, which, lasting for an hour or more, had been mistaken for death. To have sought a medical explanation for this phenomenon would
15　have been held by Silas himself, as well as by his minister and fellow-members, a wilful self-exclusion from the spiritual significance that might lie therein. Silas was evidently a brother selected for a peculiar discipline, and though the effort to interpret this discipline was discouraged by the absence, on his part, of any spiritual vision during his outward trance, yet it was believed by himself and others that its
20　effect was seen in an accession of light and fervour.

1 **opinion** = the beliefs or views of a group or majority of people (*ODE*)
2 **had presented**　present = exhibit, show
3 **as that of every fervid nature must be**　as =「…するように、…と同様に（〈様態〉を表す）」 that は 2 行目の inward life を指す。must be の後には a history and a metamorphosis が省略されている。
3 **nature**　前に修飾語を伴って「…の性質の人」の意味になる。cf. mind や soul などにも同じような用法がある。a noble mind =「高潔な人」 a brave soul =「勇敢な人」
4 **condemned** = doomed　condemn [kəndém]
6 **marked**　mark = characterize, distinguish
6 **an artisan early incorporated in …** = an artisan (who was) early incorporated in … If someone or something is incorporated into a large group, system, or area, they become a part of it. (*COBUILD*)
6 **a narrow religious sect**　特定されていないが、サイラスがかつて属していた非国教徒の宗派の一つ。10 行目の the church assembling がその宗教集団を指す。非国教徒とは、英国国教会に属さず、独自の宗教活動を行う英国のプロテスタントのこと。
7 **layman**「平信徒」
7 **distinguishing himself by**　distinguish oneself by … =「…で名をあげる、有名になる」
7 **gifts**　gift = a natural ability or talent (*ODE*)
8 **at the very least**　cf. at least
8 **weight** = importance, influence
13 **suspension of consciousness**「一時的な意識喪失状態」 suspension = breaking off, interruption
13 **had been mistaken for death**　mistake A for B =「A を B と間違える、思い違いをする」
14 **To have sought a medical explanation for this phenomenon would have been held …**　主語に仮定の意味が含まれている仮定法過去完了。If 節を用いて書き換えると、If they had sought a medical explanation for this phenomenon, it would have been held … となる。
14 **would have been held**　hold A (to be) B =「A を B だと考える、みなす」 ここでは受動態になっている。B に当たるのが 16 行目の a wilful self-exclusion。
15 **minister**「（プロテスタント教会における）牧師、聖職者」
16 **a wilful self-exclusion from …**「…を故意に自ら排除すること」
17 **evidently**「見たところ、どうやら…らしい」 e.g. Evidently Mrs Smith thought differently.（どうやら、スミス夫人の考えは違うらしかった。）(*ODE*)
17 **brother**「信徒、信者仲間」 cf. 24 ページ 7 行目の brethren
17 **discipline** = instruction imparted to disciples or scholars; teaching; learning; education, schooling *Obs.* (*OED*)「修養、修業」
18 **on his part**　on one's part =「…の側で（に）」 e.g. There is no need for any further instructions on my part.（私の側では、これ以上の指示は必要ありません。）(*COBUILD*)
18 **spiritual vision**　spiritual については 19 ページ 5 行目の注を参照。COBUILD において vision は the experience of seeing something that other people cannot see と説明されており、その具体的な一例として宗教的経験 (a religious experience) が挙げられている。 e.g. Some women reported seeing the saint in a vision.（何人かの女性がその聖人の幻影を見たと報告した。）
20 **accession**「増加、増大」

ランタン・ヤードにいた頃、サイラスにはウィリアム・デイン (William Dane) という親友がいた。対照的な性格の二人は、信仰についての話題に興じる間柄だった。サイラスに発作が生じた時、ウィリアムはそれを悪魔の訪れのようだと警告する。サイラスにはセアラ (Sarah) という婚約者がいたが、彼女は何やら動揺している様子が窺えた。

　その頃、教会の老執事が重い病気にかかり、信者たちは毎晩交代で看病することになった。当番の夜にサイラスは発作を起こして意識を失い、その間に執事は息を引き取ってしまう。加えて、同夜に教会の金が盗まれる事件が生じ、現場にはサイラスのナイフが残されていた。一連の状況から、サイラスは嫌疑をかけられてしまう。助けの言葉を求めるサイラスに対するウィリアムの態度は冷淡なものだった。教会は神の裁きを得るためにくじを引く手段を講じ、その結果サイラスの有罪を確定した。ウィリアムの奸計に気づいたサイラスは、彼を問いつめた。

Part 2

"The last time I remember using my knife, was when I took it out to cut a strap for you. I don't remember putting it in my pocket again. *You* stole the money, and you have woven a plot to lay the sin at my door. But you may prosper, for all that: there is no just God that governs the earth righteously, but a God of lies, that bears witness against the innocent."

There was a general shudder at this blasphemy.

William said meekly, "I leave our brethren to judge whether this is the voice of Satan or not. I can do nothing but pray for you, Silas."

Poor Marner went out with that despair in his soul—that shaken trust in God and man, which is little short of madness to a loving nature. In the bitterness of his wounded spirit, he said to himself, "*She* will cast me off too." And he reflected that, if she did not believe the testimony against him, her whole faith must be upset as his was. . . . We are apt to think it inevitable that a man in Marner's position should have begun to question the validity of an appeal to the divine judgment by drawing lots; but to him this would have been an effort of independent thought such as he had never known; and he must have made the effort at a moment when all his energies were turned into the anguish of disappointed faith. If there is an angel who records the sorrows of men as well as their sins, he knows how many and deep are the sorrows that spring from false ideas for which no man is culpable.

Marner went home, and for a whole day sat alone, stunned by despair, without any impulse to go to Sarah and attempt to win her belief in his innocence.

翌日、サイラスは不信心の念から逃れるため、いつものように織機の仕事に向かった。セアラはサイラスとの婚約を破棄し、それからひと月も経たぬうちにウィリアムと結婚した。ほどなくしてサイラスはランタン・ヤードを去ったのだった。

1 **strap**「皮ひも」

3 **a plot** = a plan or project, secretly contrived by one or more persons, to accomplish some wicked, criminal, or illegal purpose (*OED*)

3 **lay the sin at my door**　lay A at B's door =「A（罪、責任、失敗など）を B に負わせる、B のせいにする」という慣用句表現。

3 **for all** = in spite of

4 **bears witness**「証言する、証を立てる」

6 **There was a general shudder**「一同に戦慄が走った」

7 **brethren**　22 ページ 17 行目に出てくる brother の複数形。*OALD* は used to talk to people in church or to talk about the members of a male religious group と説明している。

8 **do nothing but ...**「ただ…するだけだ、…しかしない」 cf. nothing but = only

10 **little short of ...**「ほとんど…で、…同然で」 short of ... =「…が不足して」という慣用句に、little =「ほとんど … ない」という否定の意味が組み合わさった表現。 e.g. His return was little short of a miracle.（彼の生還はほとんど奇跡だった。）

10 **a loving nature**　23 ページ 3 行目の注を参照。

11 ***She*** = Sarah

13 **as his was** = as his whole faith (in God and man) was upset

13 **We are apt to think it inevitable that ...**　be apt to =「…する傾向にある、…しがちである」 it は形式目的語で、その内容は後続の that 節（名詞節）を指す。

14 **should have begun**　仮定法過去完了。この箇所を if 節で書き換えると、if a man had been in Marner's position, he should have begun to question … となる。should は「当然…するはずだ」という推量の意味。

15 **drawing lots**　lot = an object (app. usually a piece of wood) used in a widely diffused ancient method of deciding disputes, dividing plunder or property, selecting persons for an office or duty, etc., by an appeal to chance or the divine agency supposed to be concerned in the results of chance (*OED*)　人間による調査ではなく、祈りを捧げつつ偶然の運 (chance) 頼みで神の手に結果をゆだねることは、カルヴァン派の神学理論に即していた。どのような手順でくじ引きが執り行われたか詳細は不明だが、サイラスは複数の棒状のもの（または別の形状のもの）の中から前もって印をつけられたものを選んだために有罪判決を下されたようである。(Oxford 版注釈 182)　後年サイラスは "there's drawing o' lots in the Bible"（原著第 16 章）と述懐しているが、くじに裁きを委ねる例としては、たとえば旧約聖書ヨナ書第 1 章 7 節に、"Come, and let us cast lots, that we may know for whose cause this evil *is* upon us" という一節がある。

15 **this**　直前の to question the validity of an appeal to the divine judgment by drawing lots を指す。

15 **would have been**　仮定法過去完了。

16 **must have made** = would have had to make (Oxford 版注釈 182)

16 **the effort**　直前の an effort of independent thought (= an effort to think independently) を指す。

19 **spring from** = are caused by, arise from

19 **culpable** = deserving blame or censure, blameworthy (*OED*)

Part 1 EXERCISES

A 以下の設問に答えなさい。

1. Why is Silas valued in Lantern Yard?

    a. Because he is a skilled artisan.

    b. Because he is a pious layman.

    c. Because he is an ardent clergyman.

    d. Because he is a serious scholar.

2. Why is Silas watched with interest in Lantern Yard?

    a. Because his fit seems mysterious.

    b. Because his personality seems dangerous.

    c. Because his discipline seems strange.

    d. Because his way of living seems unacceptable.

3. What does the word "therein" in line 16 refer to?

    a. In the prayer-meeting

    b. In the death

    c. In the explanation

    d. In the phenomenon

B 原文の中であなたが重要だと思ったキーワードやキーフレーズを二つ選び、それらを書き出しなさい。また、それらを選んだ理由について、それぞれ日本語で簡潔に説明しなさい。

    1.   キーワードやキーフレーズ (　　　　) 行目

       理由

    2.   キーワードやキーフレーズ (　　　　) 行目

       理由

Part 2 EXERCISES

A 以下の設問に答えなさい。

1. Which of the following statements is true?
    a. Drawing lots is a fairly reliable method to receive God's message.
    b. Though Silas feels himself betrayed, he still believes William.
    c. There are only several ears that listen to Silas's insistence.
    d. Silas's unexpected sacrilege triggers other people's shock.

2. Why does William respond to Silas "meekly" in line 7?
    a. Because William is almost certain about the strength of his own religious faith.
    b. Because William is feeling his brethren's hostile attitudes towards himself.
    c. Because William is making himself look innocent, being conscious of his triumph.
    d. Because William is concerned about Silas's mental disorder, feeling pity for him.

3. What is it that Silas does not lose in the passage?
    a. Friendship   b. Money   c. Faith   d. Fame

B 原文の中であなたが重要だと思ったキーワードやキーフレーズを二つ選び、それらを書き出しなさい。また、それらを選んだ理由について、それぞれ日本語で簡潔に説明しなさい。

1. キーワードやキーフレーズ (　　　　) 行目

   理由

2. キーワードやキーフレーズ (　　　　) 行目

   理由

Unit 1～2 (原著第1章) の全体のあらすじを、自分の言葉で600～800字程度の日本語に要約しなさい。四つの英文箇所の内容に留意し、これらを適切な形で組み込むこと。

Unit 3　Silasが執心する機（はた）と金

▌原著第2章▐

　ランタン・ヤードから移り住んだ新たな土地ラヴィロウは、自然のままの風景や人々の素朴でのんびりとした暮らしぶりなど、サイラスにとってまったく異なる環境だった。ランタン・ヤードにあった神への信仰に溢れた敬虔な生活習慣はそこにはなく、サイラスは失意の過去とは無縁の暮らしを送ることとなった。

Part 1

　His first movement after the shock had been to work in his loom; and he went on with this unremittingly, never asking himself why, now he was come to Raveloe, he worked far on into the night to finish the tale of Mrs Osgood's table-linen sooner than she expected—without contemplating beforehand the money she would put
5　into his hand for the work. He seemed to weave, like the spider, from pure impulse, without reflection. Every man's work, pursued steadily, tends in this way to become an end in itself, and so to bridge over the loveless chasms of his life. Silas's hand satisfied itself with throwing the shuttle, and his eye with seeing the little squares in the cloth complete themselves under his effort. Then there were the calls of hunger;
10　and Silas, in his solitude, had to provide his own breakfast, dinner, and supper, to fetch his own water from the well, and put his own kettle on the fire; and all these immediate promptings helped, along with the weaving, to reduce his life to the unquestioning activity of a spinning insect. He hated the thought of the past; there was nothing that called out his love and fellowship toward the strangers he had
15　come amongst; and the future was all dark, for there was no Unseen Love that cared for him. Thought was arrested by utter bewilderment, now its old narrow pathway was closed, and affection seemed to have died under the bruise that had fallen on its keenest nerves.

　オズグッド夫人のテーブル掛けを仕上げたサイラスは、金貨で報酬を受け取る。金貨を触ったり眺めたりする行為は、彼に喜びをもたらした。以前なら金には信仰や慈善のためという目的が伴っていたが、あらゆる目的が失われた今、金は欲望を育む土壌となった。
　その頃、サイラスが隣人たちと親しくなれるかに思える出来事があった。村の女が病にかかった際、彼はかつての自分の母親にならって薬草から薬を作り、それを彼女に与えて治してやったのだ。これにより村人たちはサイラスを頼るようになったが、結局サイラスは彼らを追い返したため、かえって溝は深まってしまった。

1 **went on with**　go on with ... = continue ...
2 **now ...**　　now (that) ... =「…となった今では、…したその時（から）」 nowは接続詞。16 行目の now も同じ用法。
3 **worked far on into the night**　work on「働き続ける」と far into the night「夜遅くまで」が合わさった形。
3 **tale** = <archaic> a number or total (*ODE*)
6 **Every man's work, pursued steadily, tends ...** = Every man's work, when it is pursued steadily, tends ...
　分詞構文が文中に挿入された形。
7 **end** = aim, object
7 **bridge over ...**　「…を埋める」「…を乗り越える」
7 **chasms**　　chasm [kǽz(ə)m] =「空白」「亀裂」
8 **shuttle**　「（織機の）杼」 縦糸の間を往復して横糸を通すもの
8 **his eye with seeing ...** = his eye (satisfied itself) with seeing ...
9 **complete themselves** = become complete; get finished
9 **the calls of hunger**　「空腹が要求するもの → 空腹の欲求」 of は主格関係を表す。Hunger called を名詞化した表現。　e.g. the rise of the sun =「太陽が昇ること → 日の出」The sun rises の名詞化表現。
11 **all these immediate promptings**　「これらすべてのじかに迫りくる欲求、衝動」　cf. prompt = urge, incite
13 **the thought of the past**　目的格関係を表す of の使い方。e.g. the love of beauty =「美を愛する心」
　この一文は He hated thinking [to think] of the past の意味。
14 **called out**　call out (vt.) = summon forth, evoke
14 **fellowship** = a feeling of friendship, companionship
15 **Unseen Love**　「目に見えない神の愛」 大文字で書かれていることから、ここは神の愛を表していると考えられる。ランタン・ヤードでの事件によって、サイラスは信仰、つまり神の愛を信じる心を失ってしまった。cf. "God is love"（新約聖書ヨハネの手紙 1 第 4 章 8 節、16 節）
16 **was arrested**　arrest = stop, check　e.g. The spread of the disease can be arrested.（その病気の蔓延は阻止することができる。）(*ODE*)
17 **had fallen on**　fall on ... =「…の身に降りかかる、…に襲いかかる」

コラム 2：　田園と都市

　サイラスが移り住んだラヴィロウは、"Merry England"（18 ページ 4 行目）と称される古き良き時代を偲ばせる田園地帯に位置する。これに対し、彼が以前に暮らしていたランタン・ヤードは、ラヴィロウの住人が "North'ard"（18 ページ 18 行目）と疎遠な呼び方をし、得体の知れぬ機織り職人サイラスの異質性と関連づけていることからも察せられるように、ラヴィロウとは対比的な形で提示されている。事実、ラヴィロウが新たな時代の声の届かぬ古くて伝統的な村であるとは対照的に、ランタン・ヤードは 18 世紀中葉の産業革命に象徴される北部の工業都市（cf. "a big town" 原著第 10 章）として設定されている。織機はその産物で、サイラスはすでにランタン・ヤード時代から用いているが（24 ページ下部のあらすじを参照）、ラヴィロウの住人からは懐疑の目を向けられる要因となる。さらに付け加えると、非国教会派プロテスタントの一見不可解な教義が前景化されたランタン・ヤードと、敬虔さには劣るものの素朴に国教会を信奉するラヴィロウという宗教的差異も、両地域のコントラストを際立たせる要素となっている。

> サイラスの金はますます増え、ためる行為そのものが目的と化すほど、彼は金にのめりこんでいった。

Part 2

He began to think it was conscious of him, as his loom was, and he would on no account have exchanged those coins, which had become his familiars, for other coins with unknown faces. He handled them, he counted them, till their form and colour were like the satisfaction of a thirst to him; but it was only in the night, when his work was done, that he drew them out to enjoy their companionship. He had taken up some bricks in his floor underneath his loom, and here he had made a hole in which he set the iron pot that contained his guineas and silver coins, covering the bricks with sand whenever he replaced them. . . .

So, year after year, Silas Marner had lived in this solitude, his guineas rising in the iron pot, and his life narrowing and hardening itself more and more into a mere pulsation of desire and satisfaction that had no relation to any other being. His life had reduced itself to the functions of weaving and hoarding, without any contemplation of an end towards which the functions tended. The same sort of process has perhaps been undergone by wiser men, when they have been cut off from faith and love—only, instead of a loom and a heap of guineas, they have had some erudite research, some ingenious project, or some well-knit theory. Strangely Marner's face and figure shrank and bent themselves into a constant mechanical relation to the objects of his life, so that he produced the same sort of impression as a handle or a crooked tube, which has no meaning standing apart. The prominent eyes that used to look trusting and dreamy, now looked as if they had been made to see only one kind of thing that was very small, like tiny grain, for which they hunted everywhere: and he was so withered and yellow, that, though he was not yet forty, the children always called him "Old Master Marner".

> しかし、サイラスがこのように萎んでいく段階にあっても、その愛情がすべて消失しまっているわけではないことを示す出来事があった。彼はラヴィロウに来て以来大切に使用していた土壺を誤って割ってしまった。サイラスは悲しい思いで破片を拾ってくっつけると、それ以降も思い出の品としてもとの場所へ置いておいたのだった。
>
> ここまでがラヴィロウに来て15年目までのサイラスの歴史である。昼は機織り、夜は貨幣との饗宴の毎日を送っていた。彼は光り輝く貨幣の山を愛し、その脳裏に浮かぶのは常に金のことばかりであった。しかし、15年目のクリスマスの頃、サイラスの人生に二度目の大きな変化が生じ、彼の生活は不可思議な形で隣人たちの生活と交じり合うことになるのである。

1　**it** = money
1　**on no account** = under no circumstances (*ODE*)
2　**familiars** = close friends, companions
4　**the satisfaction of a thirst**　目的格関係を表す of の使い方。29 ページ 13 行目の注を参照。本ページ 12 行目の any contemplation of an end も同様。
4　**it was only in the night ... that he drew them out**　強調構文。
7　**guineas**　「ギニー（金貨）」　an old British gold coin or unit of money worth 21 shillings (*OALD*)　*OED* によると、1663 年から 1813 年まで鋳造された。shilling については 35 ページ 5 行目の注を参照。
8　**replaced them** = put them back
9　**his guineas rising in the iron pot**　独立分詞構文。ここは等位接続詞を用いて置き換えられ、and his guineas had risen in the iron pot となる。rise = increase in number, size, amount, or degree (*ODE*)
10　**his life narrowing and hardening itself more and more into a mere pulsation of desire and satisfaction**　同じく独立分詞構文。「彼の暮らしはますます狭く無感覚なものになっていき、ただ欲望と満足が脈打っているにすぎない状態と化していた」
13　**an end towards which the functions tended**　end については 29 ページ 7 行目の注を参照。tend (to/ towards ...) = take a particular direction (*OALD*)
15　**only ... they have had some erudite research,** ～　「ただし、彼らには学問の研究や～がある」　only は「ただし、だがしかし」という意味で、接続詞的に使われる。
16　**well-knit theory**　「よくまとめられた理論、整然たる理論」　knit [nít]
18　**so that ...**　「その結果 ...」　結果の so that の前にはコンマがあり、後続の動詞には（原則として）助動詞を伴わず、意味的にはすでに現れた結果を表すことが多い。(『英文法解説』392)
18　**the same sort of impression as a handle or a crooked tube**　「取っ手や曲がった管（が生み出すの）と同じ類の印象」　crooked [krúkid]。
19　**has no meaning standing apart**　「それだけ別に切り離しては意味をなさない」　この場合の stand は「…（の状態・関係・立場）である」という意味で、be 動詞に近い。
22　**he was so withered and yellow, that ... the children always called him "Old Master Marner"**　so ... that ～ =「とても ... なので～」　結果や程度を意味する接続詞で、18 行目の so that ... とは区別。Old Master Marner =「マーナー爺さん」　Master は一般に労働者階級の男性に対して、または彼らの間で用いられる呼称。(『方言研究』534)

コラム 3：　薬草と土壺

　この Unit のあらすじ箇所に書かれた薬草と土壺のエピソードは、ランタン・ヤードの事件以来失われたかに見えるサイラスの人間性が、完全に枯渇しているわけではないことを窺わせるものである。両者に共通するのは、過去に培った愛情とその記憶である。病にかかった女に同情心を感じた彼は、母親譲りの薬草の知識によって彼女を救い、その際、ラヴィロウに来て初めて "a sense of unity between his past and present life"（原著第 2 章）を感じている。また、ラヴィロウに来て以来愛用し、誤って割ってしまった土壺を所持し続けた理由は "for a memorial"（同章）と記されている。薬草や母親への言及は物語後半にもなされ、また、Unit 10 Part 2 には上記の引用に似た "a consciousness of unity between his past and present" という表現も登場するので、今後も引き続き着目してほしい

Part 1 EXERCISES

A 以下の設問に答えなさい。

1. Which of the following statements is not true?
    a. It is nothing but weaving that Silas clings to after the shocking incident.
    b. The spider image of Silas emphasizes the flexible nature of his weaving.
    c. Silas cannot suppress the natural demands of his appetite.
    d. Nothing inspires in Silas any affection for his neighbours.

2. According to the passage, what happens to Silas after he moves to Raveloe?
    a. Accumulating money becomes less important than connection to society.
    b. His daily behaviour becomes lively, compared with that in Lantern Yard.
    c. His past becomes what he actually wants to bring to mind.
    d. He becomes unable to experience any deepening in thought.

3. What is this passage mainly about?
    a. Silas's deepening illusion in Raveloe
    b. Silas's self-conscious effort in Raveloe
    c. Silas's closed existence in Raveloe
    d. Silas's reflection on his inner self in Raveloe

B 原文の中であなたが重要だと思ったキーワードやキーフレーズを二つ選び、それらを書き出しなさい。また、それらを選んだ理由について、それぞれ日本語で簡潔に説明しなさい。

1. キーワードやキーフレーズ (　　　　　) 行目

   理由

2. キーワードやキーフレーズ (　　　　　) 行目

   理由

Part 2 EXERCISES

A 以下の設問に答えなさい。

1. Which of the following statements is true?
    a. Silas's solitude is closely related to his lack of economic satisfaction.
    b. Silas has an objective strong enough to make use of his money.
    c. Silas and wiser men are acquainted with each other for a certain period.
    d. Silas's accumulation of money and his life's reductive process occur simultaneously.

2. What change occurs to Silas's appearance over the years?
    a. It gives the impression of some sort of mechanical object.
    b. It becomes nothing worth looking at for a long time.
    c. His eyes come to focus on objects in the distance.
    d. He is regarded as very advanced in years by half the villagers.

3. What does the passage say Silas and wiser men have in common?
    a. Some scholarly pursuit
    b. A weaving machine
    c. Lack of belief
    d. A large amount of money

B 原文の中であなたが重要だと思ったキーワードやキーフレーズを二つ選び、それらを書き出しなさい。また、それらを選んだ理由について、それぞれ日本語で簡潔に説明しなさい。

1. キーワードやキーフレーズ (　　　　) 行目

   理由

2. キーワードやキーフレーズ (　　　　) 行目

   理由

Unit 4　Cass 家の兄弟 Godfrey と Dunsey

▮原著第 3 章▶

　ラヴィロウで一番の大立者は地主カス (Squire Cass) で、「赤屋敷」(the Red House) と呼ばれる大きな邸宅に住んでいた。妻は亡くなって久しかった。妻と母の役割を担う人間がいないおかげで、地主カスは金離れのいい暮らしをし、二人の息子はそれぞれ性質に問題をかかえていた。とりわけ、賭け事や飲酒が好きで自堕落な次男のダンスタン (Dunstan)、通称ダンシー (Dunsey) の評判は悪かった。跡継ぎの長男ゴドフリー (Godfrey) は立派で気立てが良かったものの、次男と同じような道を歩む心配があった。そうなれば、彼は周囲から期待される花嫁候補のナンシー・ラミター (Nancy Lammeter) を失いかねない。最近のゴドフリーはなぜか顔色がさえなかった。

　サイラス・マーナーがラヴィロウに暮らして 15 年目となる 11 月末のある日の午後、ゴドフリーは酒に酔って帰宅したダンシーと対峙する。ゴドフリーは以前弟に手渡してしまった小作人の地代を返せと要求するが、ダンシーはこれをのらりくらりと拒否した。本来この地代は父に渡すはずのものだったのだ。

Part 1

　Godfrey bit his lips and clenched his fist. "Don't come near me with that look, else I'll knock you down."

　"Oh no, you won't," said Dunsey, turning away on his heel, however. "Because I'm such a good-natured brother, you know. I might get you turned out of house and
5　home, and cut off with a shilling any day. I might tell the Squire how his handsome son was married to that nice young woman, Molly Farren, and was very unhappy because he couldn't live with his drunken wife, and I should slip into your place as comfortable as could be. But you see, I don't do it—I'm so easy and good-natured. You'll take any trouble for me. You'll get the hundred pounds for me—I know you
10　will."

　"How can I get the money?" said Godfrey, quivering. "I haven't a shilling to bless myself with. And it's a lie that you'd slip into my place: you'd get yourself turned out too, that's all. For if you begin telling tales, I'll follow. Bob's my father's favourite—you know that very well. He'd only think himself well rid of you."

15　"Never mind," said Dunsey, nodding his head sideways as he looked out of the window. "It 'ud be very pleasant to me to go in your company—you're such a handsome brother, and we've always been so fond of quarrelling with one another, I shouldn't know what to do without you. But you'd like better for us both to stay at home together; I know you would. So you'll manage to get that little sum o' money,
20　and I'll bid you good-bye, though I'm sorry to part."

2 **else** = or else = otherwise
3 **turning away on his heel**　turn on one's heel = turn away suddenly, esp. angrily or rudely (*LDCE*)
4 **might get you turned …, and cut off …**　might は仮定法の用法で、以降のダンシーの言葉に現れる種々の過去形助動詞も同様。get + A + p.p. = 「Aを…させる、Aが…されるようにする」e.g. get the soldiers sent back to the battlefield（兵士たちを戦場へ戻らせる）12 行目の get yourself turned out も同じ用法。turn … out (of/from ～) = force … to leave a place (*OALD*)
4 **house and home**　「家、家庭」（強意）
5 **cut off with a shilling**　cut … off with a shilling =「申しわけに 1 シリングだけ遺産を与えて…を勘当する」shilling は 1971 年まで用いられていた英国の通貨単位で、20 分の 1 ポンドに当たる。1 pound = 20 shillings = 240 pence　cf. cut … off without a penny とも言う。pence は penny の複数形。31 ページ 7 行目の注も参照。
5 **how … = that …**　tell や see などの後に続いて「…ということ」の意味の従属節を作る。
7 **slip into your place** = smoothly replace you as an heir
7 **as comfortable as could be**　as … as can be =「この上なく…」
9 **take any trouble**　take trouble = take pains　take the trouble to (do) というように動詞を伴う表現もある。
11 **haven't a shilling to bless myself with**　cf. not have a penny to bless oneself with =「びた一文持っていない」　この表現は、bless oneself「（十字を切って）自らを祝福する、神の祝福を祈る」という言い回しに関連する。*OED* は in allusion to the cross on the silver penny (cf. Ger. *Kreuzer*), or to the practice of crossing the palm with a piece of silver と解説し、具体的な用例として『サイラス・マーナー』のこの箇所を挙げている。昔の銀貨には十字架が掘ってあったこと、あるいは幸運を祈って手のひらに銀貨で十字を切るという習慣があったことが、上記表現の背景にある。
13 **telling tales**　tell tales =「秘密を漏らす、告げ口をする」
13 **Bob's my father's favourite**　ボブとは地主(スクワイア)カスの三男。ゴドフリーとダンシーの弟。原著では第 11 章に登場する。
14 **He'd only think himself well rid of you** = He would only think himself very lucky to be rid of you（研究社版注釈 250）
16 **'ud** = would　[w] の音が脱落する方言の例。同様に will は 'ull と表記される。（『方言研究』109）
16 **in your company**　in A's company = in the company of A = together with A
18 **I shouldn't know …** = I wouldn't know …　イギリス英語の一人称では、will (would) の代わりに shall (should) を使うことがある。e.g. "When will you come back?" "I shall be late."　この shouldn't は仮定法（4 行目の注を参照）。
19 **o'** = of　[v] の音が脱落する方言の例。（『方言研究』149-50）
20 **part** = leave

コラム 4：　階級

　英国は今でも階級社会だと言われるが、階級を巡る英国特有の制度や文化は、時代を問わず様々な文学作品において登場する。本小説に登場するカス家は、地主(スクワイア)としてラヴィロウの共同体で一目置かれる存在である。地主(スクワイア)の詳細については Part 2 の 11 行目の注を参照してもらいたいが、ゴドフリーは長男ゆえ、世襲制のもと、由緒ある出自の家系を受け継ぎ維持する責務を負っており、この事実がこの Unit で展開される兄弟確執の背景にある。

　また、階級制度と切り離せないのが相続制度である。Unit 6 Part 2 ではゴドフリーが entail（限嗣相続）のあり方を巡って父から威嚇される場面が出てくるが、後に読む際には着目してもらいたい。本小説において金を巡る問題はサイラス・プロットに留まらないのである。

> 金は工面できないとゴドフリーはつっぱねた。ダンシーは飼い馬のワイルドファイアーを売ればいいとけしかけ、さらにナンシーのことに言及することによってゴドフリーの気持ちを逆なでした。

Part 2

Godfrey stood, still with his back to the fire, uneasily moving his fingers among the contents of his side-pockets, and looking at the floor. That big muscular frame of his held plenty of animal courage, but helped him to no decision when the dangers to be braved were such as could neither be knocked down nor throttled. His natural irresolution and moral cowardice were exaggerated by a position in which dreaded consequences seemed to press equally on all sides, and his irritation had no sooner provoked him to defy Dunstan and anticipate all possible betrayals, than the miseries he must bring on himself by such a step seemed more unendurable to him than the present evil. The results of confession were not contingent, they were certain; whereas betrayal was not certain. From the near vision of that certainty he fell back on suspense and vacillation with a sense of repose. The disinherited son of a small squire, equally disinclined to dig and to beg, was almost as helpless as an uprooted tree which, by the favour of earth and sky, has grown to a handsome bulk on the spot where it first shot upward. Perhaps it would have been possible to think of digging with some cheerfulness if Nancy Lammeter were to be won on those terms; but, since he must irrevocably lose *her* as well as the inheritance, and must break every tie but the one that degraded him and left him without motive for trying to recover his better self, he could imagine no future for himself on the other side of confession but that of "'listing for a soldier"—the most desperate step, short of suicide, in the eyes of respectable families. No! he would rather trust to casualties than to his own resolve— rather go on sitting at the feast and sipping the wine he loved, though with the sword hanging over him and terror in his heart, than rush away into the cold darkness where there was no pleasure left. The utmost concession to Dunstan about the horse began to seem easy, compared with the fulfilment of his own threat.

---

1 **fire** = fireplace
3 **held** 19ページ5行目の注を参照。
3 **when the dangers to be braved were such as could neither be knocked down nor throttled**「対処すべき危険の要因が殴り倒せたり絞め殺せたりできるようなものではなかった場合」 brave ... = have to deal with something difficult or unpleasant in order to achieve something (*OALD*)　such as ... =「…のようなもの」
4 **natural** = innate
6 **press** (vi.) = push one's way roughly, esp. in a mass (*LDCE*)

6 **on all sides** = from all quarters

6 **his irritation had no sooner provoked him to defy Dunstan ... than the miseries ... seemed more unendurable to him ...**　no sooner ... than 〜 =「…するとすぐに〜した」　e.g. I had no sooner finished washing my car than it started raining.（車を洗い終わったとたんに、雨が降り出した。）provoke ... to do =「…を駆り立てて〜させる」

8 **step** = measure, action

10 **From ...**「…からは離れて、逃れて」前に away などを補って考える。

10 **fell back on**　fall back on = resort to

11 **a small squire**「小地主」地主 (landowner) には大規模な地所を所有する貴族と、小規模な地所を所有する地方地主が含まれ (Aidan Cruttenden, *The Victorians* (London: Evans, 2003) 36)、小地主と呼ばれる地主カスは後者に分類される。原著第3章では、"He was only one among several landed parishioners"（彼は何人かいる土地持ちの教区民の一人にすぎなかった）、"Squire Cass had a tenant or two"（地主カスは一人か二人の小作人を使っていた）などと描写されている。squire = a country gentleman or landed proprietor, *esp.* one who is the principal landowner in a village or district (*OED*)

12 **equally disinclined to dig and to beg**「（土地、畑を）掘り起こすことにも、施しを乞うことにも、同じように嫌気がさしている」cf. 新約聖書ルカによる福音書第16章3節 "I cannot dig; to beg I am ashamed."

14 **shot**　shoot = sprout

14 **it would have been possible to think of digging with some cheerfulness if Nancy Lammeter were to be won on those terms**　would have been は仮定法過去完了。if ... were to 〜は仮定法過去に属するが、未来の実現可能性が乏しい仮定を表す。cf. 条件節と帰結節で時制が異なる例。If he were kind, he would have helped you a long time ago.（もし彼が親切なら、とっくの昔に君を助けていたろうに。）→ 親切でないという事実は（過去もそうだったが）現在でも変わらないという含意。terms =「条件」なお、このあたりから自由間接話法 (free indirect speech) という技法が用いられている。40ページのコラム5を参照。

16 **but** = except　18行目も同様。

18 **on the other side of confession**「告白の彼方に、告白を行ってしまった後」

19 **'listing for a soldier** = enlisting as a soldier　これは財政的窮境に陥ったり家族と不和になったりした良家の若者にとって最後の手立てであった。(Oxford版注釈 183)

19 **short of ...**　COBUILD には以下の説明がある。Short of a particular thing means except for that thing or without actually doing that thing.

20 **respectable families**「良家」respectable = of good or fair social standing, and having the moral qualities regarded as naturally appropriate to this (*OED*)　cf. ヴィクトリア朝小説においてはしばしば "respectability" という概念が前景化する。cf. Walter Allen, *The English Novel: A Short Critical History* (London: Dent, 1954) 135-39.

20 **he would rather trust to casualties than to his own resolve**　would rather ... than 〜 =「〜するくらいなら…する方がいい」e.g. I would rather stay home than go out for dinner.　casualties = chances, chance occurrences

21 **with the sword hanging over him**「常に身に迫る一触即発の危険な状態」を意味する sword of Damocles [dǽməkliːz] または Damocles' sword（ダモクレスの剣）という表現によるもの。*OED* には used by simile of an imminent danger, which may at any moment descend upon one と説明されている。古代ギリシアの都市シラクサの僭主ディオニュシオス1世（Dionysius I, 430-367 B.C.）の廷臣ダモクレスが王者の幸福をたたえたので、王がある宴席でダモクレスを王座につかせ、その頭上に毛髪1本で抜き身の剣をつるし、王者には常に危険がつきまとっていることを悟らせたというギリシアの説話にちなむ。（『ブリタニカ国際大百科事典』）sword の w は発音しないことにも留意。

24 **his own threat**　この Part 2 の直前に、苛立ったゴドフリーが、自分がすべてを父に話せばお前はおしまいだぞとダンシーを脅す場面がある。

Part 1 EXERCISES

A 以下の設問に答えなさい。

1. Why does Dunsey confidently tell Godfrey to get the money himself?
    a. Because Dunsey knows it is hard for Godfrey to resist his brother's blackmail.
    b. Because Dunsey has a certain belief in brotherly love.
    c. Because Dunsey is already sure of his acquisition of his brother's inheritance.
    d. Because Dunsey believes himself so good-natured as to be pitied by his brother.
2. What is true about Godfrey's married life?
    a. He is not happy though it is running smoothly enough.
    b. He dislikes its somewhat convenient aspects.
    c. He regrets having brought about his wife's degradation.
    d. He is concerned about its disclosure to his father.
3. What is the current condition of Godfrey and Dunsey?
    a. They share the goal of their discussion.
    b. It is possible to separate them from each other.
    c. Dunsey has a sense of superiority over his brother.
    d. Godfrey expects his brother's secret to be revealed.

B 原文の中であなたが重要だと思ったキーワードやキーフレーズを二つ選び、それらを書き出しなさい。また、それらを選んだ理由について、それぞれ日本語で簡潔に説明しなさい。

1.　キーワードやキーフレーズ (　　　　) 行目

　　理由

2.　キーワードやキーフレーズ (　　　　) 行目

　　理由

Part 2 EXERCISES

A 以下の設問に答えなさい。

1. What information is not given concerning Godfrey's character?
   a. He prefers taking his chances to making choices.
   b. He is weak in that he fails to adhere to his moral beliefs.
   c. His irritableness helps him maintain his position against Dunsey.
   d. His indecisiveness makes him unfit to confront troubles.

2. What will not happen to Godfrey after "all possible betrayals" in line 7?
   a. Loss of his pride   b. Loss of his terror   c. Loss of his status   d. Loss of his bride

3. What does the phrase "the one" in line 17 refer to?
   a. The tie with Squire Cass   b. The tie with Dunsey   c. The tie with Nancy   d. The tie with Molly

4. What is it that Godfrey does not think of as a literal choice?
   a. Committing suicide   b. The sword hanging over him
   c. 'Listing for a soldier   d. Digging and begging

B 原文の中であなたが重要だと思ったキーワードやキーフレーズを二つ選び、それらを書き出しなさい。また、それらを選んだ理由について、それぞれ日本語で簡潔に説明しなさい。

1. キーワードやキーフレーズ (　　　　) 行目

   理由

2. キーワードやキーフレーズ (　　　　) 行目

   理由

Unit 3 〜 4 (原著第 2 〜 3 章) の全体のあらすじを、自分の言葉で 600 〜 800 字程度の日本語に要約しなさい。四つの英文箇所の内容に留意し、これらを適切な形で組み込むこと。

（あらすじの続き）

　　ワイルドファイアーの売却をしぶしぶ承諾したゴドフリーは、その役目をダンシーに託した。ダンシーは部屋を出ていき、残されたゴドフリーは自身の状況を苦々しく考えた。
　　26歳のゴドフリーがした秘密の結婚は、彼の人生を蝕む病毒であった。卑しい情熱と気の迷い、そして気の迷いからの覚醒という忌まわしい物語であった。彼はそれが一部ダンシーのわなだということを知っていたが、同時に自分の不道徳な愚行にも原因があったのだ。将来の妻としてこの4年間想いを寄せてきたナンシーを諦めねばならず、さらに、秘密が暴露されれば父の激しい怒りを買うことになり、自らの立場を失うことになるだろうと懸念するのだった。

▼原著第4章▼

　　翌朝、ダンシーはワイルドファイアー売却のために猟場へ出かけた。途中で「石切場」(the Stone-pit) と呼ばれる地所にあるサイラスの小屋のそばを通った時、彼が大金を隠し持っている噂を思い出した。猟場で知人たちとの売却交渉を取りまとめた後、ダンシーは持ち馬の柵越えの技を誇示しようとし、誤ってワイルドファイアーを死なせてしまう。金もうけの手立てをなくした彼は、酒を飲んで毒づき、猟場を後にした。
　　霧と黄昏の薄暗さが増す中、ダンシーはサイラスの小屋にやってくる。彼はサイラスから金を手に入れる算段でいた。霧は雨に変わった。小屋に明かりはついていたが、サイラスは不在だった。ダンシーは床下に隠してあった金貨の革袋を見つけ出し、それを盗んで、雨の降る暗闇の中へと去っていった。

コラム5：　自由間接話法（描出話法）

　　Unit 4 Part 2 の中ほどから、表面上は三人称の地の文でありながら、ゴドフリーの内面に入り込み、彼の考えが前面に浮き上がるような描写がなされている。このような語りの手法を自由間接話法 (free indirect speech) あるいは描出話法 (represented speech) という。『ロイヤル英文法』は描出話法について、「He said … などを表現しないで、被伝達部を独立させて地の文の中に埋め込んで、発言者の言葉を伝達者の言葉のようにして述べる話法で、修辞的な技法の1つ。時制の一致や代名詞の人称などはふつうの間接話法と同じであるが、疑問文の語順などは直接話法のままであることが多い」(737) と説明している。他の話法と比較してみよう。
　　・He said, "How can I marry her?" （直接話法 direct speech）
　　・He asked how he could marry her. （間接話法 indirect speech）
　　・How could he marry her? （自由間接話法・描出話法）
この技法はもちろんエリオットの創作ではないが、彼女は初期作品よりこれを意識的に多用している。本作品ではこれ以降も自由間接話法がたびたび用いられ、登場人物の内面の意識や心理が浮き彫りにされているので、各場面における機能や効果について引き続き着目してもらいたい。

1. loom (17ページ4行目)

2. winnowing machine (17ページ5行目)

3. flail (17ページ5行目)

4. treadmill (17ページ9行目)

5. turnpike (19ページ7行目)

6. bonnet (73ページ8行目)

1. 出典：ウィキメディア・コモンズ（Wikimedia Commons）
2. Benjamin Butterworth, *The Growth of Industrial Art* (New York: Knopf, 1972) 24.
   出典：ゲッティ イメージズ（Getty Images）
4. "Britannica on the Treadmill," *Encyclopædia Britannica* 27 Oct. 2014, 5 May 2017 <https://www.britannica.com/topic/Britannica-on-the-treadmill-1998450>.
   出典：ゲッティ イメージズ（Getty Images）
5. Ben Weinreb and Christopher Hibbert eds., *The London Encyclopædia* (London: Macmillan, 1983) 895.
   出典：ゲッティ イメージズ（Getty Images）

Unit 5　予期せぬ事件と Silas の心理

原著第 5 章

> ダンシーが金貨を盗んで姿をくらました頃、サイラスは小屋の近くまで戻ってきていた。夕食前に翌日用のより糸がないことに気づき、これを求めに出かけていたのだ。いつもの習慣から、彼は何の心配も抱くことなく小屋に入り、体を温めた。そして、夕食を食べながらテーブルに並べた金貨を眺める楽しみに浸ろうと考えた。

Part 1

He rose and placed his candle unsuspectingly on the floor near his loom, swept away the sand without noticing any change, and removed the bricks. The sight of the empty hole made his heart leap violently, but the belief that his gold was gone could not come at once—only terror, and the eager effort to put an end to the
5　terror. He passed his trembling hand all about the hole, trying to think it possible that his eyes had deceived him; then he held the candle in the hole and examined it curiously, trembling more and more. At last he shook so violently that he let fall the candle, and lifted his hands to his head, trying to steady himself, that he might think. Had he put his gold somewhere else, by a sudden resolution last night, and
10　then forgotten it? A man falling into dark waters seeks a momentary footing even on sliding stones; and Silas, by acting as if he believed in false hopes, warded off the moment of despair. He searched in every corner, he turned his bed over, and shook it, and kneaded it; he looked in his brick oven where he laid his sticks. When there was no other place to be searched, he kneeled down again and felt once more
15　all round the hole. There was no untried refuge left for a moment's shelter from the terrible truth.

　　Yes, there was a sort of refuge which always comes with the prostration of thought under an overpowering passion: it was that expectation of impossibilities, that belief in contradictory images, which is still distinct from madness, because
20　it is capable of being dissipated by the external fact. Silas got up from his knees trembling, and looked round at the table: didn't the gold lie there after all? The table was bare. Then he turned and looked behind him—looked all round his dwelling, seeming to strain his brown eyes after some possible appearance of the bags where he had already sought them in vain. He could see every object in his cottage—and
25　his gold was not there.

3 **made his heart leap**　If you say that your heart leaps, you mean that you experience a sudden, very strong feeling of surprise, fear, or happiness.　e.g. My heart leaped at the sight of her.（彼女の姿を見て、私は胸がどきんとした。）(COBUILD)　cf. My heart leaps up when I behold / A rainbow in the sky（空に虹を見る時わが心は躍る）── ウィリアム・ワーズワース (William Wordsworth, 1770-1850) の詩 "The Rainbow" の冒頭。『サイラス・マーナー』原著のエピグラフには、ワーズワースの詩 "Michael" の一節が用いられている。69 ページのコラム 10 も参照。

6 **his eyes had deceived him**　deceive = mislead　e.g. The boys, if my eyes did not deceive me, were praying.（私の見間違いでないなら、その少年たちは祈りを捧げていた。）(COBUILD)

7 **curiously** = carefully, attentively, *arch.* (*OED*)

7 **let fall the candle** = let the candle fall

8 **that he might think** = so that he might think = in order that he might think　目的を表す副詞節。

9 **Had he put his gold somewhere else … and then forgotten it?**　直接話法で書き換えれば、"Did I put my gold somewhere else … and then forget it?" となる。40 ページの自由間接話法に関するコラム 5 を参照。21 行目の didn't the gold lie there after all? も自由間接話法。

13 **kneaded**　knead [níːd]

13 **sticks**　「たきぎ、薪」

15 **There was no untried refuge left**　「まだ試していない逃げ場など残っていなかった、あらゆる逃げ場を探しつくした」　cf. leave no … untried ＝「あらゆる…をやってみる」

17 **with the prostration of thought under an overpowering passion**　「強烈な感情のもとに思考力が屈して、感情に圧倒されて思考力が衰え」

18 **that expectation of impossibilities**　目的格関係を表す of の使い方。29 ページ 13 行目の注を参照。

23 **after** = in pursuit or quest of (*ODE*)

24 **in vain** = without success or a result (*ODE*)。

（あらすじの続き）

> サイラスは絶叫し、しばらくして落ち着くと、織機のところへ座り込んだ。盗難の可能性に思い当り、それは人間の手の届かぬ残酷な力によるものかといったんは思ったが、その後、村人のジェム・ロドニー（22 ページのあらすじを参照）の仕業だという考えに至った。降りしきる雨の中、彼は被害を訴えるため、村のお歴々が集っているであろう居酒屋兼宿屋「虹亭」（19 ページ 20 行目の注を参照）へと急ぎ足で向かった。

▼ **原著第 6 章** ▶

> この章では、虹亭で村人たちが交わす地元の様々な話題が紹介される。自由闊達な談話が飛び交い、最後には昔から伝わる幽霊のことに話が及ぶ。

原著第7章

> それまで話題となっていた幽霊かと見まがうばかりの姿でサイラスが虹亭に現れると、一同は驚愕した。彼はそこにいたジェム・ロドニーに盗難の件で食ってかかった。興奮したサイラスをとりなした村人たちは、彼の話に耳を傾けた。

Part 2

Silas now told his story, under frequent questioning as the mysterious character of the robbery became evident.

This strangely novel situation of opening his trouble to his Raveloe neighbours, of sitting in the warmth of a hearth not his own, and feeling the presence of faces and voices which were his nearest promise of help, had doubtless its influence on Marner, in spite of his passionate preoccupation with his loss. Our consciousness rarely registers the beginning of a growth within us any more than without us: there have been many circulations of the sap before we detect the smallest sign of the bud.

The slight suspicion with which his hearers at first listened to him, gradually melted away before the convincing simplicity of his distress: it was impossible for the neighbours to doubt that Marner was telling the truth....

"It isn't Jem Rodney as has done this work, Master Marner," said the landlord. "You mustn't be a-casting your eye at poor Jem. There may be a bit of a reckoning against Jem for the matter of a hare or so, if anybody was bound to keep their eyes staring open, and niver to wink; but Jem's been a-sitting here drinking his can, like the decentest man i' the parish, since before you left your house, Master Marner, by your own account."

"Ay, ay," said Mr Macey; "let's have no accusing o' the innicent. That isn't the law. There must be folks to swear again' a man before he can be ta'en up. Let's have no accusing o' the innicent, Master Marner."

Memory was not so utterly torpid in Silas that it could not be wakened by these words. With a movement of compunction as new and strange to him as everything else within the last hour, he started from his chair and went close up to Jem, looking at him as if he wanted to assure himself of the expression in his face.

"I was wrong," he said—"yes, yes—I ought to have thought. There's nothing to witness against you, Jem. Only you'd been into my house oftener than anybody else, and so you came into my head. I don't accuse you—I won't accuse anybody—only," he added, lifting up his hands to his head, and turning away with bewildered misery, "I try—I try to think where my guineas can be."

5 **promise** = a sign, or a reason for hope that something may happen, especially something good (*OALD*)
6 **rarely ... any more than ~** 「…でないのは～でないのとほとんど同じだ」 cf. not ... any more than ~ = no more ... than ~ =「… でないのは～でないのと同じだ、～（がそうでないの）と同様に…でない」という慣用句の類似表現。 e.g. A whale is not a fish any more than a horse is. = A whale is no more a fish than a horse is.（クジラが魚でないのは、馬が魚でないのと同じだ。）以下の各表現とは区別せよ。
  no less ... than ~ =「～と同じく … だ」
   e.g. She is no less happy than he.（彼女は彼と同じく幸せだ。）
  not more ... than ~ =「～ほど … でない」
   e.g. She is not more happy than he.（彼女は彼ほど幸せでない。）
  not less ... than ~ =「～に勝るとも劣らず … だ」
   e.g. She is not less happy than he.（彼女は彼に勝るとも劣らず幸せだ。）
また、73 ページ 6 行目の注も参照。
7 **registers** = records
7 **without** = outside　この意味で用いられるのは文語的で、通例 within と対をなす。
12 **It isn't Jem Rodney as has done this work**　as は who, which, that などの関係代名詞や接続詞 that の代わりに用いられる方言。（『方言研究』208-09, 236, 345）この文は強調構文。
13 **a-casting** = casting　a- は現在分詞の前につく方言。（『方言研究』283-86）　15 行目の a-sitting も同様。
13 **reckoning** = the avenging or punishing of past mistakes or misdeeds (*ODE*)　Jem は密猟者 (poacher)（原著第 5 章）であるため。
14 **matter**　「問題、件」
15 **niver** = never　[e] を [i] と発音する方言。原著では他に cliver (=clever)、dillicate (=delicate)（第 16 章）などの例がある。（『方言研究』30, 554）
15 **i' the parish** = in the parish　方言で、前置詞 in, on, upon などは、それに強勢がない場合は [n] が発音されない。（『方言研究』121）
16 **by your own account**　account = description, report　cf. by all accounts = according to what everyone says (*LDCE*)
17 **o' the innicent** = of the innocent　o' については 35 ページ 19 行目の注を参照。innicent = innocent　無強勢の中間音節や閉音節は、各種の母音が [i] となることが多い。（『方言研究』95-97, 497）
18 **again'** = against（『方言研究』324-25）
18 **ta'en** [te:n]= taken（『方言研究』57, 657-58）　take up = seize by legal authority, arrest, apprehend (*OED*)
21 **With a movement of compunction as new and strange to him as everything else within the last hour**　同等比較 as ... as ～「～と同じくらい…である」の句が a movement of compunction を修飾している。compunction = a feeling of guilt or moral scruple that prevents or follows the doing of something bad (*ODE*)
25 **Only**　31 ページ 15 行目の注を参照。26 行目の only も同様。

（あらすじの続き）

> 　村人たちはサイラスのために事件の解決策を思案した。巡査のところへ行って、自分たちの誰か一人を巡査代理に任命してもらおうという話になったが、その人選を巡ってひと悶着が起きる始末だった。結局、その後サイラスは二人の村人と連れだって巡査のもとへ出かけていった。

Part 1 EXERCISES

A 以下の設問に答えなさい。

1. Which of the following statements is true?
    a. Silas realizes the fact of the theft immediately.
    b. Silas searches his cottage rather half-heartedly.
    c. Silas makes every effort only to find himself helpless.
    d. Silas finds a shelter to save himself from his sin.

2. Put the following statements into correct time order.
    a. Silas takes every possible area into consideration.
    b. Silas disbelieves his vision.
    c. Silas resigns himself to what seems to be beyond possibility.
    d. Silas attempts to calm down in order to consider the situation.
    e. Silas realizes something different in the hole.
    f. Silas's trembling makes him drop his candle.
    g. Silas asks himself if the previous day's memory has been lost.
    (　)→(　)→(　)→(　)→(　)→(　)→(　)

3. What is this passage mainly about?
    a. Silas's composed state of mind
    b. Silas's desperate struggle for discovery
    c. Silas's doubt about possibilities
    d. Silas's effortless search for gold

B 原文の中であなたが重要だと思ったキーワードやキーフレーズを二つ選び、それらを書き出しなさい。また、それらを選んだ理由について、それぞれ日本語で簡潔に説明しなさい。

1.　キーワードやキーフレーズ (　　　　) 行目

　　理由

2.　キーワードやキーフレーズ (　　　　) 行目

　　理由

Part 2 EXERCISES

A 以下の設問に答えなさい。

1. What is new to Silas in this passage?
    a. He is given a chance to reflect on his fault.
    b. He is annoyed by the villagers' manner of questioning.
    c. His obsession with gold is shaken off.
    d. His presence of mind is totally disturbed.

2. What advice does Mr Macey give to Marner?
    a. It is possible not to doubt the innocent.
    b. It is possible to judge who is innocent.
    c. It is good to avoid criticizing the innocent.
    d. It is good to swear a charge against the innocent.

3. What is this passage mainly about?
    a. Silas's painful embarrassment
    b. Silas's step to recovery
    c. Silas's discourse with nature
    d. Silas's continual revival

4. In line 20, what memory is considered to come back to Silas?
    a. That of Jem Rodney
    b. That of Silas's mother
    c. That of Raveloe
    d. That of Lantern Yard

B 原文の中であなたが重要だと思ったキーワードやキーフレーズを二つ選び、それらを書き出しなさい。また、それらを選んだ理由について、それぞれ日本語で簡潔に説明しなさい。

1. キーワードやキーフレーズ (　　　) 行目

   理由

2. キーワードやキーフレーズ (　　　) 行目

   理由

Unit 6　Godfrey と父 Squire Cass の葛藤

原著第 8 章

> 翌朝、村全体が盗難の話に沸き立った。ゴドフリーも加わって捜索がなされる中、泥に埋もれた火打ち箱が見つかった。虹亭の亭主がこの火打ち箱と以前にやってきた行商人とを関連づけたため、行商人犯人説の是非が議論されたが、ゴドフリーはこれを相手にしなかった。
> 　ゴドフリーの関心は、盗難ではなくダンシーとワイルドファイアーにあった。弟の消息不明が気がかりだった彼は、ダンシーから馬を買う取り決めをしていた知人により、馬の事故死の一件について知らされた。知人と別れたゴドフリーは思案する。

Part 1

　Godfrey rode along slowly, representing to himself the scene of confession to his father from which he felt that there was now no longer any escape. The revelation about the money must be made the very next morning; and if he withheld the rest, Dunstan would be sure to come back shortly, and finding that he must bear
5 the brunt of his father's anger, would tell the whole story out of spite, even though he had nothing to gain by it. There was one step, perhaps, by which he might still win Dunstan's silence and put off the evil day: he might tell his father that he had himself spent the money paid to him by Fowler; and as he had never been guilty of such an offence before, the affair would blow over after a little storming. But
10 Godfrey could not bend himself to this. He felt that in letting Dunstan have the money, he had already been guilty of a breach of trust hardly less culpable than that of spending the money directly for his own behoof; and yet there was a distinction between the two acts which made him feel that the one was so much more blackening than the other as to be intolerable to him.
15 　"I don't pretend to be a good fellow," he said to himself; "but I'm not a scoundrel—at least, I'll stop short somewhere. I'll bear the consequences of what I *have* done sooner than make believe I've done what I never would have done. I'd never have spent the money for my own pleasure—I was tortured into it."

> ゴドフリーは父に事情を打ち明ける際のうまいやり方について考えを巡らせた。地主(スクワイア)カスは厳格な男だった。怒りのあまり決断すると、怒りが静まってもその決断を止めようとはしなかった。害悪を放任しておきながら、いよいよという段になって、情け容赦のなさを発揮するのだった。ゴドフリーは真夜中近くまで父への対応策を考えていたが、明朝目を覚ますとその考えは失われていた。いつものように都合の良い偶然に頼る気持ちが蘇り、状況を今のままにしておくのが賢明だと思った。

1 **representing to himself**　represent = bring clearly and distinctly before the mind, esp.(to another) by description or (to oneself) by an act of imagination (*OED*)
2 **The revelation about ... must be made**　make a revelation about ... =「…について事実を明らかにする」 e.g. The biographer made a shocking revelation about the writer's personal life.（伝記作者は作家の私生活について衝撃的な事実を明らかにした。）この文以降は自由間接話法。40 ページのコラム 5 を参照。
3 **withheld**　withhold = hide
4 **bear the brunt of ...**　「…の矢面に立つ」 e.g. The CEO is bearing the brunt of the criticisms against his company.（その経営者は会社に対する非難の矢面に立っている。）
5 **spite** = malice, hatred, ill will
6 **step**　37 ページ 8 行目の注を参照。
7 **put off the evil day** = postpone something unpleasant for as long as possible (*ODE*)　put off the evil hour という言い方もある。
8 **Fowler**　地主カスの領地に住む小作人の名前。地代をゴドフリーに預けた。34 ページのあらすじを参照。(スクワイア)
9 **blow over** = (of storms or storm-clouds) to pass over a place without descending upon it; to pass away, come to an end; also *fig.* of misfortune, danger, etc. (*OED*)
9 **storming**　storm = complain with rough and violent language; rage (*OED*)
10 **bend himself to this**　bend A to B = force A to submit to B
11 **a breach of trust hardly less culpable** = a breach of trust (which had been) hardly less culpable
11 **hardly less culpable than ...**　否定語と劣等（劣勢）比較の組み合わせに注意。
12 **for his own behoof**　behoof = <archaic> benefit or advantage (*ODE*)　for の代わりに in, on, to などの前置詞が用いられることもある。
13 **the one ... the other ...**　通常は the one = the former（前者）、the other = the latter（後者）だが、この場合は、the one = spending the money directly for his own behoof、the other = letting Dunstan have the money となる。(研究社版注釈 277)
13 **so much more blackening than the other as to be intolerable to him**　程度・結果を表す so ... as to do =「～するほどに…な、とても…なので～する」の構文と、比較級の much more ... than ～ が合わさった形になっている。cf. He was so foolish as to leave the door unlocked.（彼は愚かにもドアに鍵をかけていなかった。）　cf. blacken = defame
16 **stop short**　If someone stops short of doing something, they come close to doing it but do not actually do it. (*COBUILD*)
17 **sooner than** = rather than
17 **make believe** = pretend
17 **what I never would have done**　仮定法過去完了「やろうなどとは夢にも思わなかっただろうこと」強調のため never が would より前に置かれている。
18 **I was tortured into it**　torture A into doing = distress and force A to do　e.g. The interrogator tortured him into confessing he had stolen the money.（取調官は彼を責め立てて金を盗んだことを白状させた。）

原著第9章

> 翌朝、ゴドフリーは父に対し、ワイルドファイアーが事故死した件と、小作人の金を弟に与えてしまった件を切り出した。

Part 2

The Squire was purple with anger before his son had done speaking, and found utterance difficult. "You let Dunsey have it, sir? And how long have you been so thick with Dunsey that you must *collogue* with him to embezzle my money? Are you turning out a scamp? I tell you I won't have it. I'll turn the whole pack of you out of the house together, and marry again. I'd have you to remember, sir, my property's got no entail on it;—since my grandfather's time the Casses can do as they like with their land. Remember that, sir. Let Dunsey have the money! Why should you let Dunsey have the money? There's some lie at the bottom of it."

"There's no lie, sir," said Godfrey. "I wouldn't have spent the money myself, but Dunsey bothered me, and I was a fool, and let him have it. But I meant to pay it, whether he did or not. That's the whole story. I never meant to embezzle money, and I'm not the man to do it. You never knew me do a dishonest trick, sir."

"Where's Dunsey, then? What do you stand talking there for? Go and fetch Dunsey, as I tell you, and let him give account of what he wanted the money for, and what he's done with it. He shall repent it. I'll turn him out. I said I would, and I'll do it. He shan't brave me. Go and fetch him."

"Dunsey isn't come back, sir."

"What! did he break his own neck, then?" said the Squire, with some disgust at the idea that, in that case, he could not fulfil his threat.

"No, he wasn't hurt, I believe, for the horse was found dead, and Dunsey must have walked off. I daresay we shall see him again by-and-by. I don't know where he is."

"And what must you be letting him have my money for? Answer me that," said the Squire, attacking Godfrey again, since Dunsey was not within reach.

"Well, sir, I don't know," said Godfrey hesitatingly. That was a feeble evasion, but Godfrey was not fond of lying, and, not being sufficiently aware that no sort of duplicity can long flourish without the help of vocal falsehoods, he was quite unprepared with invented motives.

2 **it** 小作人 Fowler から預かった地代のこと。Part 1 の 8 行目の注を参照。
3 **thick** = close in confidence and association; intimate, familiar (*OED*)
3 *collogue* = collude = work together secretly or illegally in order to trick other people (*OALD*)
3 **Are you turning out a scamp?** turn out = prove to be, become   scamp = (*old-fashioned*) a child who enjoys playing tricks and causing trouble (*OALD*)
4 **won't have it**   COBUILD には以下の説明がある。You can use have in expressions such as 'I won't have it' or 'I'm not having that', to mean that you will not allow or put up with something.
4 **I'll turn the whole pack of you out of the house together**   3 行目注の turn out との意味の違いに注意。15 行目も同様。この turn out については 35 ページ 4 行目の注を参照。
5 **I'd have you to remember** = I wish you would remember (研究社版注釈 279)
6 **entail** = legal settlement which restricts the right of a property-owner to sell it or bequeath it to anyone he chooses (Oxford 版注釈 185) 「限嗣相続、限定相続」とは、長男のみが相続者となる長子相続 (primogeniture) とともに、支配的土地所有家族が自らの所有地を無傷で代々子孫に受け継がせるための制度である。相続者が不動産を売却したり分割したり抵当に入れたりすることを防ぐため、その相続権に制限をつける。これにより次の世継ぎへの土地財産譲渡が確保される。詳しくは、Daniel Pool, *What Jane Austen Ate and Charles Dickens Knew: From Fox Hunting to Whist—the Facts of Daily Life in Nineteenth-Century England* (New York: Simon, 1993) 89-94 を参照。
12 **never knew me do …**   never knew ... (to) do = have never known ... (to) do =「…したためしを知らない」 この箇所の do は原形不定詞。
13 **What do you stand talking there for?**   what … for = for what reason = why   14 行目と 22 行目も同様。
15 **He shall repent it**   主語が二人称あるいは三人称の場合に用いられる shall は、話者の意志を表し、「…させる」の意味。ここは I will make him repent it と同義。直後の He shan't brave me の shall も同じ用法。
25 **no sort of duplicity can long flourish without the help of vocal falsehoods**   no ... without 〜の二重否定の構文になっており、結果的に「声をそれらしく偽れば、いかなる二枚舌もずっとうまく通用する」という肯定の意味と同じになる。

(あらすじの続き)

　ゴドフリーの父は怒りが収まらず、何か他に隠された事情があるのではないかと息子を問い詰めた。さらに、ナンシー・ラミターとの結婚話が進まないことに触れ、無粋で情けないゴドフリーを非難した。いずれについてもゴドフリーは必死に言い逃れしたが、父は聞く耳を持たず、その憤りは最後まで続いた。このような調子で何とか会見は終わったものの、ゴドフリーはナンシーの件で新たな不安に駆られるのだった。そこでまた彼は、都合の良い偶然にすがりつくという、いつもの隠れ家へと逃げ込むのであった。

Part 1 EXERCISES

A 以下の設問に答えなさい。

1. Which of the following statements is true?
    a. Godfrey feels it inevitable to hurt his father.
    b. Godfrey thinks his confession is sure to end Dunsey's life.
    c. Godfrey thinks of confessing to counteract Dunsey.
    d. He tries to protect himself by consoling his father.
2. What idea is it that Godfrey cannot accept?
    a. That Dunsey has broken silence.
    b. That Dunsey has survived all perils.
    c. That Godfrey has spent money for his father.
    d. That Godfrey has given way to Dunsey
3. How does Godfrey think of himself in the second paragraph?
    a. He has a responsible mind.
    b. He has a selfish view of life.
    c. He is an admired gentleman.
    d. He is a wicked villain.

B 原文の中であなたが重要だと思ったキーワードやキーフレーズを二つ選び、それらを書き出しなさい。また、それらを選んだ理由について、それぞれ日本語で簡潔に説明しなさい。

1. キーワードやキーフレーズ (   ) 行目

    理由

2. キーワードやキーフレーズ (   ) 行目

    理由

Part 2 EXERCISES

A 以下の設問に答えなさい。

1. What is this passage mainly about?
    a. Godfrey's violent hatred towards his father's statement
    b. Godfrey's desperate struggle for predominance over his father
    c. The Squire's silent rage about his sons' ungratefulness
    d. The Squire's stubborn reaction to his sons' thoughtlessness

2. What is not true about the Squire?
    a. He does not like to leave his first son's fault as it is.
    b. His distrust in his second son is temporarily suspended.
    c. He does not easily stop finding fault with either of his sons.
    d. His threat of disinheritance arises from his indignation.

3. What is true about Godfrey?
    a. He successfully convinces his father of his brother's guilt.
    b. His self-justification is too well-founded to leave any room for doubt.
    c. He feels himself cornered in spite of his vain attempts at self-protection.
    d. His resorting to deceit bothers him because of his vocal falsehoods.

B 原文の中であなたが重要だと思ったキーワードやキーフレーズを二つ選び、それらを書き出しなさい。また、それらを選んだ理由について、それぞれ日本語で簡潔に説明しなさい。

1. キーワードやキーフレーズ (　　　) 行目

   理由

2. キーワードやキーフレーズ (　　　) 行目

   理由

Unit 5〜6 (原著第5〜9章) の全体のあらすじを、自分の言葉で600〜800字程度の日本語に要約しなさい。四つの英文箇所の内容に留意し、これらを適切な形で組み込むこと。

Unit 7　村の女性 Dolly と Nancy

▼原著第 10 章▶

　サイラスの盗難事件に進展はなかった。行商人探しも功を奏しなかった。ダンシーがいなくなった件と、同日に起きた盗難事件とを結びつける者は皆無で、これはゴドフリーも同じだった。サイラスは金に執心するという目的を失い、空虚感に打ちひしがれていた。
　だが彼はすっかり見捨てられていたわけではなかった。サイラスに対する村人たちの気持ちが、今までより優しいものに変化していたのである。たとえば、仕立て屋で教区教会書記のメイシー氏（44 ページに登場）は好意を示そうとサイラスを訪問し、晴れ着を仕立てて教会に来るように勧めた。
　車大工の妻ドリー・ウィンスロップ (Dolly Winthrop) も同様だった。良心的で善良で健全な彼女は、7 歳になる幼い息子のエアロン (Aaron) を連れ、脂菓子を持参してサイラスの小屋を訪ねる。サイラスは今や、助けは外から来るに違いないと感じ、村人を見るとその善意に頼りたいというかすかな意識が生じていた。ドリーは熱心にサイラスを教会へと誘うが、彼は教会のことは知らないし行ったことがないと答えた。

Part 1

　But now, little Aaron, having become used to the weaver's awful presence, had advanced to his mother's side, and Silas, seeming to notice him for the first time, tried to return Dolly's signs of goodwill by offering the lad a bit of lard-cake. Aaron shrank back a little, and rubbed his head against his mother's shoulder, but still
5　thought the piece of cake worth the risk of putting his hand out for it.
　"O, for shame, Aaron," said his mother, taking him on her lap, however; "why, you don't want cake again yet awhile. He's wonderful hearty," she went on, with a little sigh—"that he is, God knows. He's my youngest, and we spoil him sadly, for either me or the father must allays hev him in our sight—that we must."
10　She stroked Aaron's brown head, and thought it must do Master Marner good to see such a "pictur of a child". But Marner, on the other side of the hearth, saw the neat-featured rosy face as a mere dim round, with two dark spots in it.
　"And he's got a voice like a bird—you wouldn't think," Dolly went on; "he can sing a Christmas carril as his father's taught him; and I take it for a token as he'll
15　come to good, as he can learn the good tunes so quick. Come, Aaron, stan' up and sing the carril to Master Marner, come."
　Aaron replied by rubbing his forehead against his mother's shoulder.
　"O, that's naughty," said Dolly, gently. "Stan' up, when mother tells you, and let me hold the cake till you've done."

1 **having become used to the weaver's awful presence**　cf. be used to = be accustomed to　to は前置詞なので、後には名詞または動名詞が来ることに注意。過去の習慣的動作や継続的状態を表す used to (do) とは区別。

3 **lard-cake**　Made of dough, lard, sugar and spice. (Penguin 版注釈 190)　当時の読者の多くにとっても馴染みのない、地方特有の食べ物だったようである。(Oxford 版注釈 186)

6 **for shame** = shame on you　(*informal*) used to say that somebody should feel ashamed for something they have said or done (*OALD*)

6 **why**　疑問詞ではなく間投詞 (interjection)。

7 **wonderful hearty** = wonderfully hearty　hearty = (of a person's appetite) robust and healthy (*ODE*)

8 **that he is**　that は指示代名詞。名詞のみならず、広く他の品詞や語群を受け、力強い陳述をなす語法。(『方言研究』665) この that は前の wonderful hearty を受ける。9 行目の that we must も同様に考える。

8 **sadly** = badly, very much

9 **allays** = always　[ɔ́ːləz] [ɔ́ləs] と発音する。方言において always の [w] が脱落する例。(『方言研究』110, 333)

9 **hev** = have　[ɛv] と発音する。エリオット作品における have の方言は他に han, hae, ha' などが用いられている。(『方言研究』259)

10 **it must do Master Marner good to see …**　it は to 不定詞以下の内容を示す仮主語。do … good = do good to … = benefit …

11 **a "pictur of a child"**　「絵に描いたような子ども」　a … of a 〜で「…のような〜」という意味になる。e.g. an angel of a girl（天使のような少女）、a mountain of a wave（山のような波）　pictur = picture　方言で、語尾をなす -ure が -ur（あるいは -ur'）となる。(『方言研究』102-03)

13 **you wouldn't think**　「とてもそんなふうには思えないでしょうが」　would は仮定法。後に so などを補って考えるとわかりやすい。

14 **carril** = carol　45 ページ 17 行目の注を参照。

14 **I take it for a token as he'll come to good, as he can learn the good tunes so quick**　二つの as はいずれも接続詞 that を代替する方言。45 ページ 12 行目の注を参照。　a token as he'll come to good の as は「…という」の意味で、as 以下は token と同格の名詞節。as he can learn the good tunes so quick は、I take it 中の仮目的語 it の内容を示す名詞節。take A for B =「A を B だと思う」　cf. take it for granted that S+V =「…を当然のことだと思う」　23 ページ 13 行目の mistake A for B も参照。

15 **Come** = Now　命令形で間投詞的な用法。cf. Come on now! C'mon!

15 **stan' up** = stand up　nd で終わる語において [d] が脱落する方言の例。(『方言研究』140-41)

（あらすじの続き）

　エアロンは澄んだ声でクリスマス祝歌(キャロル)を歌う。ドリーはこの調べがサイラスを教会へと誘ってくれるものと思ったが、そのような効果はもたらさなかった。二人が帰ると、サイラスは安堵する。人間の愛の泉や、神の愛に対する信仰の泉はまだ閉ざされたままだったのだ。こうして彼はクリスマスを孤独に過ごした。

　ラヴィロウ村ではクリスマスの鐘が陽気に鳴り、教会にはいつも以上に人が集った。カス家の赤屋敷は家族だけの集まりだった。地主(スクワイア)カスがその歓待ぶりを発揮するのは、大みそかの大舞踏会であった。

◤原著第11章▶

> 大みそかの日。ナンシーは赤屋敷へ到着する。ゴドフリーが出迎えたが、彼女は最近自分に対してよそよそしく不可解な態度を見せる相手に不満を抱いていた。彼女は貴婦人として必要な資質というものを備えていた。同時に、少し高慢で厳しい面があった。だが、不心得な恋人に対して変わらぬ想いを抱く女性でもあった。舞踏会が始まるまで、ナンシーは姉のプリシラ(Priscilla)や伯母のオズグッド夫人他を交え、あてがわれた寝室で様々な話題に興じる。
>
> 大広間で隣席へとエスコートするゴドフリーを見ると、ナンシーは教区で最も地位ある青年の若奥様となる可能性について改めて考え、内心穏やかではなかった。息子の様子に気を揉んだ地主(スクワイア)カスは、ナンシーの父に向かってしきりに彼女への賛辞を述べ立てる。やがて舞踏会が始まった。ゴドフリーとナンシーは最初のダンスを終えた後、二人で話をする。

Part 2

"... You know one dance with you matters more to me than all the other pleasures in the world."

It was a long, long while since Godfrey had said anything so direct as that, and Nancy was startled. But her instinctive dignity and repugnance to any show of
5 emotion made her sit perfectly still, and only throw a little more decision into her voice as she said—

"No, indeed, Mr Godfrey, that's not known to me, and I have very good reasons for thinking different. But if it's true, I don't wish to hear it."

"Would you never forgive me, then, Nancy—never think well of me, let what
10 would happen—would you never think the present made amends for the past? Not if I turned a good fellow, and gave up everything you didn't like?"

Godfrey was half conscious that this sudden opportunity of speaking to Nancy alone had driven him beside himself; but blind feeling had got the mastery of his tongue. Nancy really felt much agitated by the possibility Godfrey's words suggested,
15 but this very pressure of emotion that she was in danger of finding too strong for her roused all her power of self-command.

"I should be glad to see a good change in anybody, Mr Godfrey," she answered, with the slightest discernible difference of tone, "but it 'ud be better if no change was wanted."

20 "You're very hard-hearted, Nancy," said Godfrey, pettishly. "You might encourage me to be a better fellow. I'm very miserable—but you've no feeling."

"I think those have the least feeling that act wrong to begin with," said Nancy, sending out a flash in spite of herself. Godfrey was delighted with that little flash, and would have liked to go on and make her quarrel with him; Nancy was so
25 exasperatingly quiet and firm. But she was not indifferent to him *yet*.

5 **still** (adv.) = motionlessly, calmly
7 **that's not known to me**　ゴドフリーの "You know" という親しげな言葉に対し、まるで相手と距離を置くかのようなナンシーの受動態表現に留意。
8 **different** (adv.) = differently
9 **let what would happen …** = whatever [no matter what] might happen　cf. let come what will [may] = 「どんなことがあっても」(『研究社新英和大辞典』)
10 **made amends for …**　make amends for … = compensate or make up for (a wrongdoing) (*ODE*)　e.g. He wanted to make amends for causing their marriage to fail.（彼らの結婚を失敗に終わらせたことに対して彼は償いをしたかった。) (*COBUILD*)
10 **Not if …**　Not は直前の否定疑問文の内容を指す。
11 **turned**　turn = become, change into
13 **had driven him beside himself**　drive = bring (someone) forcibly into a specified negative state (*ODE*)　e.g. His attitude drove me crazy.（彼の態度は頭にきた。）　beside oneself = 「我を忘れて、逆上して」
13 **had got the mastery of …**　get the mastery of … =「…を支配する、…より優位に立つ」
15 **this very pressure of emotion that she was in danger of finding too strong for her**　関係代名詞 that の先行詞 this very pressure of emotion は、関係詞節の中では finding の目的語に相当する。finding (this very pressure of emotion) too strong for her = 「(この感情の圧力を)自分には抗えないほど強いと感じる」
16 **roused**　rouse [ráuz]
17 **should**　35 ページ 18 行目の注を参照。
18 **'ud**　35 ページ 16 行目の注を参照。
18 **was wanted** = was necessary, was required
20 **might …**　「…くらいしてもよさそうなものだ」非難の気持ちを表す用法。　e.g. You might at least say you are sorry.（ごめんなさいくらい言ってもいいでしょ。）(『ロイヤル英文法』442)
22 **those … that act wrong** = the people … who act wrongly
22 **to begin with** = at the outset, as the first thing to be considered (*OED*)
23 **a flash**　「(感情、機知、考えなどの)ひらめき、突発」　e.g. a flash of inspiration =「とっさにわき起こる霊感」(『研究社新英和大辞典』)
23 **in spite of herself**　「思わず、自分の意に反して」

コラム 6：　季節の設定

　この Unit ではクリスマスや大みそかがクローズアップされているが、日本とは違ってこの二つは決して別物ではない。クリスマスがキリスト降誕祭であることは言うまでもないが、英国で Christmastide と言えば 12 月 24 日のクリスマス・イブから 1 月 6 日の Epiphany（公現祭）までを指し、Part 2 の大みそかの日もまさにこの季節に含まれるのである。12 月 25 日をもってクリスマスの季節を終わりとする日本の風習とは異なることに留意すべきである。

　大みそかに開催される赤屋敷の華やかな舞踏会は、当時の地主やそれに近い身分の人々がこの季節をいかに過ごしていたかを窺い知る機会を読み手に与えてくれる。さらに、この集まりは、Unit 5 の原著第 6〜7 章を中心に登場した居酒屋兼宿屋「虹亭」における村人たちの集まりの延長線上に位置づけることができる。両者に共通するのは、どちらもラヴィロウという共同体の縮図を示しており、そこに集う人々は村で生じる出来事や人間関係に対して様々なコメントを提示するという、いわゆるコーラス (chorus) の役割を担っている点である。関心のある人は、両場面で繰り広げられる対話の数々を、実際に原著で確認してもらいたい。

Part 1 EXERCISES

A 以下の設問に答えなさい。

1. Which of the following statements is not true?
    a. Both Dolly and her husband make much of Aaron.
    b. Dolly wants Aaron to sing to suit Silas's tastes.
    c. Aaron is unwilling to approach Silas.
    d. Dolly scolds Aaron for his greediness.

2. Why does Silas see Aaron's face as "a mere dim round, with two dark spots in it" in line 12?
    a. Because he feels it resembles a mask.
    b. Because he criticizes its monotonous atmosphere.
    c. Because he cannot see it clearly.
    d. Because he regards it as flat.

3. What is it that Dolly does not appreciate in Aaron?
    a. His performance
    b. His utterance
    c. His voice
    d. His beauty

B 原文の中であなたが重要だと思ったキーワードやキーフレーズを二つ選び、それらを書き出しなさい。また、それらを選んだ理由について、それぞれ日本語で簡潔に説明しなさい。

1. キーワードやキーフレーズ (　　　　) 行目

　　理由

2. キーワードやキーフレーズ (　　　　) 行目

　　理由

Part 2 EXERCISES

A 以下の設問に答えなさい。

1. Which of the following statements is true?

    a. Nancy becomes so anxious that she accepts Godfrey's words without delay.

    b. Nancy's agitation is tremendous enough to make her reveal her real nature.

    c. Nancy mostly manages to govern herself though she feels her mind affected.

    d. Nancy attaches greater importance to Godfrey's change than to his consistency.

2. What does not occur in Godfrey?

    a. The joy of having discovered a small way out

    b. The will to make up for his past deeds

    c. A sense of duty as a promising fiancé

    d. An involuntary impulse to express himself

3. What is this passage mainly about?

    a. Godfrey's firm resolution to triumph over Nancy

    b. Nancy's never-ending ill will towards Godfrey

    c. Godfrey and Nancy's unpredictable good will

    d. Godfrey's persistent attempt at reconciliation

B 原文の中であなたが重要だと思ったキーワードやキーフレーズを二つ選び、それらを書き出しなさい。また、それらを選んだ理由について、それぞれ日本語で簡潔に説明しなさい。

1. キーワードやキーフレーズ (　　　　) 行目

　　理由

2. キーワードやキーフレーズ (　　　　) 行目

　　理由

Unit 8　幼子の出現

原著第12章

> ゴドフリーがナンシーと戯れていた頃、彼の妻モリーは幼い子供を抱いて、雪に覆われた道を赤屋敷へと向かっていた。彼女との結婚を後悔し、薄情な態度を示す夫への復讐を以前から計画していたのだ。貧困と堕落の生活に加え、モリーはアヘンにも手を出していた。
>
> 道中でまたもやアヘンに頼った彼女は、サイラスの小屋の近くに来たところで昏睡状態に陥る。残された子供は、小屋の明かりに引き寄せられ、よちよち歩きで中に入ると、暖かい炉辺で眠り込んでしまう。この時サイラスは小屋にいた。しかし、いつものように戸口を開けて外を眺めているうちに例の持病の発作に襲われ、硬直して意識を失っていたのだった。やがて彼は意識を回復する。

Part 1

　　When Marner's sensibility returned, he continued the action which had been arrested, and closed his door, unaware of the chasm in his consciousness, unaware of any intermediate change, except that the light had grown dim, and that he was chilled and faint. He thought he had been too long standing at the door and looking
5　out. Turning towards the hearth, where the two logs had fallen apart, and sent forth only a red uncertain glimmer, he seated himself on his fireside chair, and was stooping to push his logs together, when, to his blurred vision, it seemed as if there were gold on the floor in front of the hearth. Gold!—his own gold—brought back to him as mysteriously as it had been taken away! He felt his heart begin to beat
10　violently, and for a few moments he was unable to stretch out his hand and grasp the restored treasure. The heap of gold seemed to glow and get larger beneath his agitated gaze. He leaned forward at last, and stretched forth his hand; but instead of the hard coin with the familiar resisting outline, his fingers encountered soft warm curls. In utter amazement, Silas fell on his knees and bent his head low to examine
15　the marvel: it was a sleeping child—a round, fair thing, with soft yellow rings all over its head. Could this be his little sister come back to him in a dream—his little sister whom he had carried about in his arms for a year before she died, when he was a small boy without shoes or stockings? That was the first thought that darted across Silas's blank wonderment. *Was* it a dream? He rose to his feet again, pushed
20　his logs together, and, throwing on some dried leaves and sticks, raised a flame; but the flame did not disperse the vision—it only lit up more distinctly the little round form of the child, and its shabby clothing. It was very much like his little sister. Silas sank into his chair powerless, under the double presence of an inexplicable surprise and a hurrying influx of memories. How and when had the child come in
25　without his knowledge? He had never been beyond the door.

1 **had been arrested**　29 ページ 16 行目の注を参照。
2 **chasm**　29 ページ 7 行目の注を参照。
3 **intermediate** = occurring or coming between two points of time or events (*OED*)
7 **blurred**　blur [bláː]
8 **Gold! …**　この一文は自由間接話法。40 ページのコラム 5 を参照。16 行目の Could this be…?、19 行目の *Was* it a dream?、24 〜 25 行目の How and when … beyond the door. も同様。
11 **restored**　restore = give (something stolen, taken away, or lost) back to the original owner or recipient (*ODE*)
13 **resisting**　cf. resistant = offering resistance to something or someone (*ODE*)　子供の巻き毛とは対照的な性質。
14 **fell on his knees**　fall on one's knees = go down on bended knee = drop the knee
15 **fair**　「色白で金髪の」 反意語は dark。原著 14 章には、モリーとその子供について "the dark-haired woman with the fair child" という描写がなされている。
15 **rings** = curls
19 **blank** = (looking) as if deprived of the faculty of speech or action (*OED*)
19 **wonderment** = astonishment
19 **rose to his feet**　rise to one's feet = stand up
23 **powerless** = powerlessly
23 **under the double presence of …**　「…という二つのもの（の存在）に圧倒されて」　cf. in the presence of …　under のニュアンスに留意。
25 **without his knowledge**　without one's knowledge =「…の知らぬ間に、…の気づかないうちに」　e.g. He crept out without his wife's knowledge.（彼は妻が気づかないうちにそっと出て行った。）（『ジーニアス英和大辞典』）

（あらすじの続き）

目を覚まして泣く子供を、サイラスは抱き上げてあやす。母親を探す様子や濡れた靴により、子供が外から来たことに気づいたサイラスは、雪の中に人が倒れているのを発見した。

コラム 7：　死と生の交錯

　赤屋敷の華やかな世界とは対照的に提示される淪落の女モリーは、社会の底辺の代表者と捉えることができる。彼女の悲惨な最期は、病や死と決して無縁ではなかった当時の社会的弱者層の危うさを間接的、象徴的に浮かび上がらせている。その死と対比的に提示されるのは幼子の生命である。サイラスはその生命を実感しているが、彼自身は、ランタン・ヤードの事件以後、"a dead man come to life again" (Unit 1 Part 2) というように、生ける屍として描写されていた。このように本小説では死と生のイメージが交錯する。そう考えると、57 ページのコラム 6 で言及した、キリスト生誕を祝うクリスマスの季節は、まさに幼子出現の舞台設定としてふさわしい。死と生に関連づけて言えば、キリストは磔刑（死）を経て、さらに復活（再生）へのプロセスを辿っている。本作品とのつながりは考えられるだろうか。

原著第 13 章

> 赤屋敷は晩餐後の余興で盛り上がっていた。突然そこへ子供を抱いたサイラスが姿を現し、一同を驚かせる。ゴドフリーは即座にそれが自分の子供であることを悟り、また、その母親つまり自分の妻はまだ死んでいないのではないかという恐怖に駆られた。子供に関する周囲からの助言をよそに、サイラスはその子を手放さないと主張した。ゴドフリーはサイラスのためにドリーを呼び出すという口実で外出し、その足で彼の住む小屋に赴くと、モリーの死を確認した。

Part 2

　He turned immediately towards the hearth, where Silas Marner sat lulling the child. She was perfectly quiet now, but not asleep—only soothed by sweet porridge and warmth into that wide-gazing calm which makes us older human beings, with our inward turmoil, feel a certain awe in the presence of a little child, such as we feel
5　before some quiet majesty or beauty in the earth or sky—before a steady glowing planet, or a full-flowered eglantine, or the bending trees over a silent pathway. The wide-open blue eyes looked up at Godfrey's without any uneasiness or sign of recognition: the child could make no visible audible claim on its father; and the father felt a strange mixture of feelings, a conflict of regret and joy, that the pulse of that little
10　heart had no response for the half-jealous yearning in his own, when the blue eyes turned away from him slowly, and fixed themselves on the weaver's queer face, which was bent low down to look at them, while the small hand began to pull Marner's withered cheek with loving disfiguration.
　"You'll take the child to the parish tomorrow?" asked Godfrey, speaking as
15　indifferently as he could.
　"Who says so?" said Marner, sharply. "Will they make me take her?"
　"Why, you wouldn't like to keep her, should you—an old bachelor like you?"
　"Till anybody shows they've a right to take her away from me," said Marner. "The mother's dead, and I reckon it's got no father: it's a lone thing — and I'm a lone thing.
20　My money's gone, I don't know where—and this is come from I don't know where. I know nothing—I'm partly mazed."
　"Poor little thing!" said Godfrey. "Let me give something towards finding it clothes."
　He had put his hand in his pocket and found half-a-guinea, and, thrusting it into Silas's hand, he hurried out of the cottage to overtake Mr Kimble.

> ゴドフリーは赤屋敷に戻った。モリーの死によって自分の忌まわしい秘密が葬られた今、彼は安堵と喜びを感じた。ナンシーとの結婚を前向きに考え直し、また、子供については養育を見守り、父親と名乗る以外は何でもしてやろうと考えていた。

2 **only soothed by sweet porridge and warmth into that wide-gazing calm**　soothe [súːð] ... into 〜 =「…をなだめて〜（の状態）にする」　e.g. The child was soothed by his mother's voice into sleep.（その子供は母親の声になだめられ、眠りについた。）　wide-gazing = gazing with her eyes wide-open

8 **claim** = demand　日本語の「クレーム」との意味のずれに注意。

9 **that ...**　同格の that で、以下の節は直前の句の内容を説明する。

13 **with loving disfiguration**　「愛着をこめて（相手の頬を）ゆがませて」

14 **the parish** = the workhouse (Oxford 版注釈 188)「救貧院」(poorhouse とも言う) は、救貧法 (Poor Law) のもと、教区 (19 ページ 2 行目の注を参照) 単位で集められた救貧税によって運営され、貧民が一定年数居住することを条件に救済措置を施される収容施設であった (井野瀬久美恵編『イギリス文化史』(昭和堂 , 2010) 69)。貧しい人が教区の扶助を受けることを go on the parish と言う。1834 年には新救貧法 (New Poor Law) が制定されたが、当時の救貧院における悲惨な生活の様子は、エリオットとほぼ同世代の作家チャールズ・ディケンズ (Charles Dickens, 1812-70) の『オリバー・トゥイスト』(*Oliver Twist*, 1837-39) に克明に描かれている。主人公の孤児オリバーが "Please, sir, I want some more" と乏しい粥のおかわりを求める場面はとりわけ有名である。

17 **Why**　55 ページ 6 行目の注を参照。

21 **mazed** = confused, bewildered (Oxford 版注釈 188)

22 **towards** = for the purpose of; for part payment or fulfilment of (*LDCE*)

23 **half-a-guinea** = half-guinea「半ギニー（金貨）」An English gold coin worth 10 shillings 6 pence, coined from the reign of Charles II to 1813 (*OED*)　guinea については 31 ページ 7 行目の注、shilling と pence については 35 ページ 5 行目の注を参照。

24 **Mr Kimble**　ゴドフリーの叔父で薬剤師。医師の免許状は持たないが、ラヴィロウの村人たちから Dr Kimble と呼ばれている。"country apothecaries in old days enjoyed that title [Doctor] without authority of diploma" (原著第 11 章) 当時の薬剤師は時に医療も行っていた。74 ページ 3 〜 5 行目も参照。

コラム 8：　共同体と共感

　57 ページのコラム 6 に記したように、赤屋敷の舞踏会は単なる舞台設定に留まらない。虹亭とのさらなる共通点は、サイラスが自身の理解力を超えた事件をきっかけに村の集まりに出向いて救いを求め、結果として共同体との対話と交流の機会が生まれることである。そのように考えれば、二つの重大事件は、それまで孤独な殻に閉じこもっていたサイラスの生き方に変化を促す触媒の役割を担っていると解釈できる。Unit 5 Part 2 の本文第 2 段落の内容を改めて想起したい。

　また、この触媒作用は双方向性を伴っている。続く原著第 14 章の第 2 段落では、"That softening of feeling towards him which dated from his misfortune ... was now accompanied with a more active sympathy, especially amongst the women" と書かれ、彼に対する村人たちの心情が、両事件によって改善されていることがわかる。本書 Introduction に記したように、エリオット文学の重要なキーワードである "sympathy" がここで用いられている点にも着目しよう。

Part 1 EXERCISES

A 以下の設問に答えなさい。

1. Which of the following statements is not true?
   a. Silas's sister's image hits him long after she passes away.
   b. The child's hair has the same colour as Silas's money.
   c. Silas's unhealthy condition makes his vision dim.
   d. Silas mistakes the child for his gold at first sight.

2. Put the following statements into correct time order.
   a. Silas thinks his lost treasure has returned.
   b. Silas is reminded of his remote past.
   c. Silas is charmed by the brightness of what he finds.
   d. Silas comes to his senses after a while.
   e. Silas realizes what he finds is alive.
   f. Silas intends to get a fire going again.
   g. Silas feels what he finds is agreeable to the touch.
   (　)→(　)→(　)→(　)→(　)→(　)→(　)

3. What is this passage mainly about?
   a. Silas's bewilderment at his lost days
   b. Silas's awakening to something lost
   c. Silas's abandonment of what is lost
   d. Silas's lost wealth regained

B 原文の中であなたが重要だと思ったキーワードやキーフレーズを二つ選び、それらを書き出しなさい。また、それらを選んだ理由について、それぞれ日本語で簡潔に説明しなさい。

1. キーワードやキーフレーズ (　　　　) 行目

   理由

2. キーワードやキーフレーズ (　　　　) 行目

   理由

Part 2 EXERCISES

A 以下の設問に答えなさい。

1. Which of the following statements is true?
   a. Godfrey does nothing but gaze at the child before talking to Silas.
   b. Godfrey is approached by the child longing for fatherly love.
   c. Silas finds himself utterly amazed by the child's response.
   d. Silas recognizes the child's distinct relation to the lost money.

2. What feeling does the author think grown-up people have when facing a small infant?
   a. Anxiety accompanying calmness
   b. Warmness aroused by impressive beauty
   c. Magnificence uninterrupted by confusion
   d. Respect mixed with fear or wonder

3. How does Godfrey betray his deceptive mind to the reader?
   a. By ignoring the child's claim
   b. By leaving the child to the weaver
   c. By taking the child to the parish
   d. By supplying the weaver with clothes

B 原文の中であなたが重要だと思ったキーワードやキーフレーズを二つ選び、それらを書き出しなさい。また、それらを選んだ理由について、それぞれ日本語で簡潔に説明しなさい。

1. キーワードやキーフレーズ (　　　　　) 行目

   理由

2. キーワードやキーフレーズ (　　　　　) 行目

   理由

Unit 7 ～ 8 (原著第 10 ～ 13 章) の全体のあらすじを、自分の言葉で 600 ～ 800 字程度の日本語に要約しなさい。四つの英文箇所の内容に留意し、これらを適切な形で組み込むこと

Unit 9　Eppie がもたらすもの

原著第14章

> その週、ラヴィロウではモリーの葬儀が行われた。子供を養おうと決意したサイラスに対し、村人たちはさらに積極的な同情を示す。とりわけドリーはかいがいしく育児の世話を買って出た。彼女の親切に感謝しながらも、サイラスは自分の手でやってやりたいと言い、子供が自分のものであることを主張した。ドリーはこれに理解を示すが、同時に、子供のために教会での洗礼命名式の必要性を説く。二人の相談の結果、子供はサイラスの母や妹と同じくヘフジバ (Hephzibah) と名づけられ、さらに短くエピー (Eppie) と呼ばれることとなった。後日、子供は教会で洗礼を受ける。

Part 1

　He had no distinct idea about the baptism and the church-going, except that Dolly had said it was for the good of the child; and in this way, as the weeks grew to months, the child created fresh and fresh links between his life and the lives from which he had hitherto shrunk continually into narrower isolation. Unlike the gold which needed nothing, and must be worshipped in close-locked solitude—which was hidden away from the daylight, was deaf to the song of birds, and started to no human tones—Eppie was a creature of endless claims and ever-growing desires, seeking and loving sunshine, and living sounds, and living movements; making trial of everything, with trust in new joy, and stirring the human kindness in all eyes that looked on her. The gold had kept his thoughts in an ever-repeated circle, leading to nothing beyond itself; but Eppie was an object compacted of changes and hopes that forced his thoughts onward, and carried them far away from their old eager pacing towards the same blank limit—carried them away to the new things that would come with the coming years, when Eppie would have learned to understand how her father Silas cared for her; and made him look for images of that time in the ties and charities that bound together the families of his neighbours. The gold had asked that he should sit weaving longer and longer, deafened and blinded more and more to all things except the monotony of his loom and the repetition of his web; but Eppie called him away from his weaving, and made him think all its pauses a holiday, re-awakening his senses with her fresh life, even to the old winter-flies that came crawling forth in the early spring sunshine, and warming him into joy because *she* had joy.

3 **from which he had ... shrunk ... into narrower isolation**　shrink = move back or away, especially because of fear or disgust (*ODE*)　cf. shrink into oneself = become withdrawn (*ODE*)
4 **hitherto** [híðətu: / hiðətúː]
5 **close-locked** = closely enclosed or shut in by locking
6 **started**　start =「はっと驚く」e.g. They started at the sound of thunder.
7 **ever-growing**　ever = always の意味で複合語を作る。10 行目の ever-repeated も同様。cf. 同じ意味の ever が単独の副詞で用いられる例：The couple lived happily ever after.
8 **making trial of ...**　make (a) trial of ... = put ... to trial =「…を試す」(『リーダーズ英和辞典』)
9 **with trust in new joy**　cf. (v.) If you trust in someone or something, you believe strongly in them, and do not doubt their powers or their good intentions. (*COBUILD*)
10 **in an ever-repeated circle**　cf. go (or run) round in circles = <infromal> do something for a long time without achieving anything but purposeless repetition (*ODE*)　round の他に around も用いられる。e.g. We've been going around in circles for an hour now.（話し合いはもうかれこれ 1 時間も堂々めぐりをしている。）(『ジーニアス英和大辞典』)
11 **compacted of ...** = composed of ... , made up of ...
14 **when Eppie would have learned to understand**　「その頃、エピーは理解するようになっているだろう」非制限用法の関係副詞節。would have learned は仮定法ではなく未来完了形で、主節との時制の一致で will が would になっている。
15 **made ...**　12 行目の forced や carried と同様に、that から始まる関係代名詞節の中の述語動詞。
15 **that time**　14 〜 15 行目の when Eppie would have learned to understand how her father Silas cared for her の内容を指す。
16 **charities**　Charity is kindness and understanding towards other people (*COBUILD*)
20 **re-awakening his senses ... even to 〜**　「彼の感覚を再び呼び起こして〜にさえ気づかせた」　cf. awake (awaken) A to B =「A に B を気づかせる」　e.g. The film helped to awaken many to the horrors of apartheid.（その映画は多くの人々にアパルトヘイト（人種隔離政策）の恐ろしさを気づかせた。）(*ODE*)

コラム 9：　洗礼と命名

　教会が司る儀式には、生誕から結婚、埋葬に至るまで様々なものがある。ここではモリーの葬儀と、後に残された娘の洗礼および命名の儀式が登場する。洗礼は、赤ん坊が水に浸されたり、頭に水を注がれることによって、信者としてキリスト教社会に受け入れられるための最初の儀式である。サイラスがエピーに母や妹と同じ名前をつけたのは奇妙に思えるかもしれないが、西洋では子供が親族の名前を継ぐ習慣は珍しくない。また、聖書に現れる名前にちなんで命名されることもよくある。ヘフジバ (Hephzibah) は、旧約聖書の列王記下第 21 章 1 節に登場する古代王国ユダの王マナセ (Manasseh) の母（先王ヒゼキア (Hezekiah) の妻）で、原義は "my delight is in her"（わが喜びは彼女にある）である。さらに、同イザヤ書第 62 章 4 節では、聖地エルサレムの別称として用いられている。

　過去のランタン・ヤードでの事件以来教会を遠ざけていたサイラスが、エピーの出現を機に教会との新たな関係が生まれ、またその過程で、命名を通して母や妹という過去の存在が彼の現在の人生に繋がるというプロット仕立てにも着目したい。31 ページのコラム 3 も参照。

> 陽光が強くなり、日も長い時分になると、サイラスとエピーが豊かな自然の中で戯れる姿が見受けられた。彼は昔なつかしい薬草を再び探し始めた。子供の成長につれ、サイラスの記憶は蘇り、麻痺していた魂は次第にはっきりとした意識を取り戻していった。
> 　3歳になったエピーはいたずらをするようになり、サイラスを当惑させる。ドリーはお仕置きを勧めるが、彼は愛するエピーに懲罰を与えることができなかった。こうして彼女はこの後も温かく育てられた。
> 　サイラスはどこへ行くにもエピーを伴い、彼女を通して周囲の世界との結びつきが育まれた。

Part 2

　Silas began now to think of Raveloe life entirely in relation to Eppie: she must have everything that was a good in Raveloe; and he listened docilely, that he might come to understand better what this life was, from which, for fifteen years, he had stood aloof as from a strange thing, wherewith he could have no communion: as some man who has a precious plant to which he would give a nurturing home in a new soil, thinks of the rain, and the sunshine, and all influences, in relation to his nursling, and asks industriously for all knowledge that will help him to satisfy the wants of the searching roots, or to guard leaf and bud from invading harm. The disposition to hoard had been utterly crushed at the very first by the loss of his long-stored gold: the coins he earned afterwards seemed as irrelevant as stones brought to complete a house suddenly buried by an earthquake; the sense of bereavement was too heavy upon him for the old thrill of satisfaction to arise again at the touch of the newly-earned coin. And now something had come to replace his hoard which gave a growing purpose to the earnings, drawing his hope and joy continually onward beyond the money.

　In old days there were angels who came and took men by the hand and led them away from the city of destruction. We see no white-winged angels now. But yet men are led away from threatening destruction: a hand is put into theirs, which leads them forth gently towards a calm and bright land, so that they look no more backward; and the hand may be a little child's.

原著第15章

> ゴドフリーはエピーの成長ぶりを陰ながら見つめていた。生得権を与えてやることはできなかったが、そのことをそれほど気にかけてはいなかった。彼の表情は以前より晴れ晴れとしていた。ダンシーのことも気にならなくなった。ゴドフリーはナンシーの家に足しげく通い、また、自分の子供たちと戯れる将来の結婚生活の幸せを思い浮かべた。そして、もう一人の子供の養育は見守ってやろう、それが父親の義務なのだからと考えた。

2 **that he might come to understand ...** that = so that　43 ページ 8 行目の注を参照。
4 **wherewith** = with which
6 **nursling**　「(特に乳母の育てる) 乳児、大事に育てられた人」が原義だが、ここでは 5 行目の a precious plant ... a new soil を指す。
7 **satisfy the wants of the searching roots**　「(滋養分を) 探し求めようとする根の欲求を満たす」
10 **irrelevant**　cf. relevant = having practical value or importance (*LDCE*)
10 **brought ... buried ...**　どちらも過去分詞。
11 **the sense of bereavement was too heavy upon him for the old thrill of satisfaction to arise again**　too ... for ... to ... の構文に留意。bereavement = loss, deprivation
16 **the city of destruction**　「滅亡の町」旧約聖書の創世記第 19 章に出てくる古代都市ソドム (Sodom) のこと。町に多くの罪悪があふれたために、神が硫黄の火を降らせて滅ぼした。作者エリオットが愛読したジョン・バニヤン (John Bunyan, 1628-88) の『天路歴程』(*The Pilgrim's Progress*, 1678) の主人公クリスチャン (Christian) が出る寓意的な旅の出発地としても登場する。(Oxford 版注釈 188)
18 **so that**　31 ページ 18 行目の注を参照。
18 **and the hand may be a little child's**　cf. 旧約聖書イザヤ書第 11 章 6 節 "and a little child shall lead them"

コラム 10：　子供の概念

　Part 2 の最終段落では子供に関する一般論的な書き方がなされている。19 世紀ヴィクトリア朝小説には数多くの子供が登場するが、そこには詩人ウィリアム・ブレイク (William Blake, 1757-1827) やウィリアム・ワーズワース (William Wordsworth, 1770-1850) らが表明したロマン主義的な無垢な子供観の影響が見て取れる。その起源はフランス啓蒙思想家ジャン＝ジャック・ルソー (Jean-Jacques Rousseau, 1712-78) にあるとされる。この子供礼賛の考え方は、43 ページ 3 行目の注で紹介したワーズワースの詩 "The Rainbow" の中の一節、"The Child is father of the Man"（子供は大人の父である）に端的に表明されている。当時こうした思想は比較的新奇なものだった。歴史家フィリップ・アリエス (Philippe Ariès) が言うように、子供は不完全な大人であるというのが従来の考え方だったとすれば、いわばこの時代には大人とは違う存在としての新たな子供像が形成されていったと言えるのである。その後この子供像は様々に形態を変えつつ 19 世紀文学に浸透していく。

　エリオットがワーズワースに心酔していたことはよく知られている。彼女は『サイラス・マーナー』のエピグラフとしてワーズワースの詩 "Michael" の一節を引用している。

　　"A child, more than all other gifts
　　That earth can offer to declining man,
　　Brings hope with it, and forward-looking thoughts."

これはまさにエピーによって導かれるサイラス像とオーバーラップする。だが、一つ留意したいのは、この詩に登場する老マイケルは、サイラスとは異なる人生を辿るという事実である。詳しくは原詩を読んでもらいたいが、そこでは、マイケルは同じように金銭的苦境を経験するものの、それに端を発して子供を手放し喪失する結果となる。この筋書きは『サイラス・マーナー』とは一見相反するように思えるが、はたしてそうだろうか。この Unit 9 で提示されたエピーを巡る二人の父親という視点を踏まえつつ Unit 10 以降を読み進めれば、ワーズワースの詩との結びつきに対する理解がさらに深まることだろう。

Part 1 EXERCISES

A 以下の設問に答えなさい。

1. What is this passage mainly about?
    a. Two similar factors that have decisive impacts on Silas
    b. Eppie's temporary interference with her foster parent
    c. Contrastive representations of the gold and the child
    d. Silas's lonesome nature lost by his reliance on wealth

2. What does Eppie not do for Silas?
    a. Enable him to weigh various alternatives
    b. Make him hold communion with nature
    c. Prevent him from staying where he used to be
    d. Give him chances to contact those around him

3. Which of the following statements is not true?
    a. Silas's hardened feelings are softened by Eppie's outgoing tendency.
    b. Eppie's interest in things new to her widens Silas's range of activities.
    c. Silas's habit of weaving is looked upon by Eppie as rather uninteresting.
    d. Without Eppie's existence Silas's moral recovery is far from realistic.

B 原文の中であなたが重要だと思ったキーワードやキーフレーズを二つ選び、それらを書き出しなさい。また、それらを選んだ理由について、それぞれ日本語で簡潔に説明しなさい。

1. キーワードやキーフレーズ (　　　　) 行目

   理由

2. キーワードやキーフレーズ (　　　　) 行目

   理由

Part 2 EXERCISES

A 以下の設問に答えなさい。

1. What happens to Silas after Eppie's appearance?
    a. Plenty of attachment to gold lingers in him despite his shock.
    b. His attention to the weather is aroused by his concern for her.
    c. His attempt to forget the theft is assisted by her counsel.
    d. He starts to free himself of his former attitudes to Raveloe life.

2. What can ① "something" and ② "hoard" in line 13 be paraphrased into respectively?
    a. ① earning ② storing
    b. ① parenting ② saving
    c. ① nurturing ② spending
    d. ② trusting ② using

3. What message does the author convey in the last paragraph?
    a. The necessity of angels' existence
    b. The difference between angels and children
    c. The warning about the threat of ruin
    d. The potential saving grace of infants

B 原文の中であなたが重要だと思ったキーワードやキーフレーズを二つ選び、それらを書き出しなさい。また、それらを選んだ理由について、それぞれ日本語で簡潔に説明しなさい。

1. キーワードやキーフレーズ (   ) 行目

    理由

2. キーワードやキーフレーズ (   ) 行目

    理由

Unit 10 16年後

原著第16章

> サイラスがエピーという新しい宝を見つけてから16年目の秋を迎えていた。日曜日の礼拝を終えた村人たちが教会から出てくる。ゴドフリーとナンシーの夫婦には経年的な変化が表れていた。帰りゆく人々の中にはサイラスらの姿もあった。

Part 1

But it is impossible to mistake Silas Marner. His large brown eyes seem to have gathered a longer vision, as is the way with eyes that have been short-sighted in early life, and they have a less vague, a more answering gaze; but in everything else one sees signs of a frame much enfeebled by the lapse of the sixteen years. The weaver's bent shoulders and white hair give him almost the look of advanced age, though he is not more than five-and-fifty; but there is the freshest blossom of youth close by his side—a blond dimpled girl of eighteen, who has vainly tried to chastise her curly auburn hair into smoothness under her brown bonnet: the hair ripples as obstinately as a brooklet under the March breeze, and the little ringlets burst away from the restraining comb behind and show themselves below the bonnet-crown. Eppie cannot help being rather vexed about her hair, for there is no other girl in Raveloe who has hair at all like it, and she thinks hair ought to be smooth. She does not like to be blameworthy even in small things: you see how neatly her prayer-book is folded in her spotted handkerchief.

That good-looking young fellow, in a new fustian suit, who walks behind her, is not quite sure upon the question of hair in the abstract, when Eppie puts it to him, and thinks that perhaps straight hair is the best in general, but he doesn't want Eppie's hair to be different. She surely divines that there is some one behind her who is thinking about her very particularly, and mustering courage to come to her side as soon as they are out in the lane, else why should she look rather shy, and take care not to turn away her head from her father Silas, to whom she keeps murmuring little sentences as to who was at church, and who was not at church, and how pretty the red mountain-ash is over the Rectory wall?

> エピーがサイラスに庭造りをしたいと言うと、すぐ後ろにいた青年エアロンが手伝いを申し出た。サイラスとエピーは自分たちの小屋に帰宅する。そこには赤屋敷から届けられた上品な家具の数々が置いてあった。しかしサイラスは、かつて土壺を愛していたのと同じように、エピーを発見した時そのままの古びた炉辺を愛していた。

1 **have gathered** = have gained
2 **as is the way with …** 「…の常として、…はいつだってそうだが」 e.g. He was showing off, as is the way with adolescent boys.（思春期の少年はいつだってそうだが、彼はこれみよがしにふるまっていた。）(*ODE*) cf. as is often the case with …
3 **answering** = responding cf. He answered her smile with one of his own.（彼は彼女の微笑みに自らの微笑みで応じた。）(*COBUILD*)
4 **frame** = a person's body with reference to its size or build (*ODE*)
6 **not more than** = at most 「せいぜい、多くても」 以下の各表現とは区別せよ。
    not less than = at least 「少なくとも」
      e.g. He has not less than 100 pounds.（彼は少なくとも 100 ポンド持っている。）
    no more than = only 「たった、わずか」
      e.g. He has no more than 100 pounds.（彼はたった 100 ポンドしか持っていない。）
    no less than = as many (much) as 「…も」
      e.g. He has no less than 100 pounds.（彼は 100 ポンドも持っている。）
  また、45 ページ 6 行目の注も参照。
7 **chastise** = correct (authoritatively) the faults of; to amend, reform, improve (a person or thing). *Obs.* (*OED*)
8 **bonnet** 婦人帽の一種。頭頂から後頭部をほとんど覆い、つけ紐をあごの下で結ぶ。顔を縁どる部分に幅広い縁（brim）を伴う場合が多く、後頭部には縁はほとんどない。10 行目 bonnet-crown の crown は帽子の山（頭を覆う部分）。41 ページの図版を参照。
13 **prayer-book** = the Book of Common Prayer 「（英国国教会または同系統教会の）祈祷書」 教会の儀式の文句や聖書からの抜粋を収めた書で、Thomas Cranmer が 1549 年に出版。その後たびたび改訂された。Thomas Cranmer はイングランド宗教改革の指導者で、新教徒として最初の Canterbury 大主教となった。(『研究社新英和大辞典』)
16 **in the abstract** 「一般的には、理論上は」 e.g. She knows poverty only in the abstract.（彼女は理屈の上でしか貧乏を知らない。）(『ジーニアス英和大辞典』) 反意表現は in the concrete。
16 **puts it to him** = puts the question to him   put a question to … = ask … a question
20 **else** 35 ページ 2 行目の注を参照。

コラム 11：   時の変化

  原著ではこの第 16 章から物語後半の第 2 部が始まる体裁となっている。第 1 部ではランタン・ヤード時代から 15 年後のラヴィロウの生活が描かれ、この第 2 部ではさらに 16 年が経過している。サイラスがそれぞれの時代に何歳だったのか改めて考えてみよう。

  こうした時の経過に呼応するように、原著第 16 章では「変化」が強調されている。次ページ下部のあらすじにあるようにエピーはエアロンから求愛されるが、彼女はこれを喜びつつも、愛するサイラスとの暮らしは変えたくないとの思いから、"I don't want any change . . . I should like to go on a long, long while, just as we are" と述べる。これに対しサイラスは、"But there's this to be thought on, Eppie: things *will* change, whether we like it or no; things won't go on for a long while just as they are and no difference" と諭す。直接の文脈からすれば、この言葉には今後さらに老いてエピーの厄介者になりたくないという彼の優しい心情が投影されているのだが、小説全体を通して見ると、変化の是非を巡るこの問題はさらに考察の価値があるだろう。Unit 2 Part 1 の 3 行目には "metamorphosis" という言葉も用いられていた。

Part 2

　　Silas had taken to smoking a pipe daily during the last two years, having been strongly urged to it by the sages of Raveloe, as a practice "good for the fits"; and this advice was sanctioned by Dr Kimble, on the ground that it was as well to try what could do no harm—a principle which was made to answer for a great deal of work in that gentleman's medical practice. Silas did not highly enjoy smoking, and often wondered how his neighbours could be so fond of it; but a humble sort of acquiescence in what was held to be good, had become a strong habit of that new self which had been developed in him since he had found Eppie on his hearth: it had been the only clew his bewildered mind could hold by in cherishing this young life that had been sent to him out of the darkness into which his gold had departed. By seeking what was needful for Eppie, by sharing the effect that everything produced on her, he had himself come to appropriate the forms of custom and belief which were the mould of Raveloe life; and as, with reawakening sensibilities, memory also reawakened, he had begun to ponder over the elements of his old faith, and blend them with his new impressions, till he recovered a consciousness of unity between his past and present. The sense of presiding goodness and the human trust which come with all pure peace and joy had given him a dim impression that there had been some error, some mistake, which had thrown that dark shadow over the days of his best years; and as it grew more and more easy to him to open his mind to Dolly Winthrop, he gradually communicated to her all he could describe of his early life.

　　ランタン・ヤードでの事件に関するサイラスの話は、ドリーの理解をはるかに超えるものだった。しかし、宗教に対するドリーの考えは、決して明晰とは言えないものの、素朴で信心深いものであった。サイラスは、人間の正しい行いと神の導きを説く彼女の言葉に次第に感化され、この世には善があり、神の摂理があるという思いに至る。
　　サイラスはエピーにも過去のことを包み隠さず話していた。自身の過去のいきさつを聞いたエピーは、亡き母についてあれこれ思いを馳せた。そして、自分が結婚する時には母の形見の指輪をはめるのだろうかと述べ、エアロンから求愛されたことを告白する。サイラスはそれを穏やかに受け入れる。

1 **had taken to**　take to = begin as a practice, habit, etc. (*LDCE*)
3 **on the ground that ...** = because ...
3 **it was as well to try**　as well = sensible, appropriate, or desirable (*ODE*)　*COBUILD* には以下の説明がある。You say it is as well to think or do something when you are advising someone to think in a particular way or to take a particular action.　e.g. It is as well to bear in mind that laughter is a great releaser of tension.（笑いは緊張を大いに和らげてくれるものだということは心に留めておいてもいい。）
4 **a principle ... in that gentleman's medical practice**　この一節に含まれる作者の皮肉に留意。that gentleman's medical practice については 63 ページ 24 行目の注を参照。
7 **held**　23 ページ 14 行目の注を参照。
9 **clew** = <archaic> a ball of thread; archaic variant of clue (*ODE*)　ギリシャ神話において、クレタ島の王ミノス (Minos) の娘アリアドネ (Ariadne) は、怪物ミノタウロス (Minotaur) 退治に来た英雄テセウス (Theseus) に恋し、彼に導きの糸を巻いた玉を持たせて、怪物を退治したあと迷宮 (Labyrinth) から脱出できるようにしてやった。（『ブリタニカ国際大百科事典』）　難問を解く鍵、糸口を「アリアドネの糸」という。ここではサイラスの職業との比喩的な関連性にも留意。
9 **hold by ...** = cling to ...
12 **appropriate** [əpróuprièit] (vt.) = take to oneself as one's own property or for one's own use (*NSOED*)　形容詞の appropriate [əpróupriət] とは意味と発音を区別。
12 **mould** = model, pattern
16 **presiding goodness** = a Power overruling all for good (研究社版注釈 320)　*OED* は goodness について、As an attribute of the Deity (said also of Christ and the Virgin Mary): Infinite benevolence, a desire for the happiness of all created beings; also the manifestation of this; beneficence と説明している。これに関連し、goodness は God の婉曲表現としても広く用いられる。e.g. Goodness knows ... = God knows ... ; in the name of goodness = in the name of God; for goodness' sake = for God's sake

---

コラム 12：　　ドリーの宗教心

　Unit 7 で登場して以来、ドリーはサイラスに常に友好的で助力を惜しまない。貧乏で無教養ではあるが、良心的で善良な精神の持ち主である。その性質は彼女の宗教心に表れている。サイラスに教会行きやエピーの洗礼を熱心に勧めるエピソードは、ドリーの信心深さを物語っている。その一方、彼女はいつも脂菓子に押す焼印 I. H. S. がキリストを意味する略語であることすら知らない。だがこうした愚かさは、滑稽ではあっても決して否定的に描かれてはいない。むしろ彼女はラヴィロウ全体の素朴な信仰の体現者として肯定的に提示されている。

　ドリーの素朴な信仰心を表す言葉を、原著第 16 章から引用しよう。"And all as we've got to do is to trusten, Master Marner—to do the right thing as fur as we know, and to trusten. For if us as knows so little can see a bit o' good and rights, we may be sure as there's a good and a rights bigger nor what we can know—I feel it i' my own inside as it must be so." （それでね、私たちがやらなくちゃいけないのは信じることだけですよ、マーナーさん—知ってる限り正しいことをやって、信じること。だって、ほとんど何にも知らない私たちだって、ちょっとばかり良いことや正しいことがわかれば、自分たちが知りうる以上に大きな良いことや正しいことがあるってはっきりわかるでしょうからね—そうに違いないって心の中で感じるんですよ。）この教えをサイラスは従順に受け入れ、さらに原著第 21 章では、ドリーが用いた上記 "trusten" という言葉を二度繰り返している（91 ページのあらすじを参照）。エピーと同様に、ドリーはサイラスの精神的再生に大きく寄与する人物なのである。ドリーの宗教心には作者の考えが何か反映されているだろうか。

Part 1 EXERCISES

A 以下の設問に答えなさい。

1. Which of the following statements is not true?
    a. Eppie's preference for tidiness causes her to feel annoyed by her hair.
    b. Silas probably has become able to see nearer than he used to.
    c. Eppie has lived for nearly one third of Silas's age.
    d. Silas's appearance makes him look older than he is.

2. Which of the following statements is true?
    a. Aaron inwardly appreciates the way Eppie's hair looks.
    b. Eppie has a full realization of Aaron's attempt to walk past her.
    c. Eppie tries in vain to avoid making eye contact with Aaron.
    d. Aaron has already mastered his courage to approach Eppie.

3. Which of the following statements is not clearly shown in the passage?
    a. Silas's and Eppie's desperate reliance on each other
    b. The introduction of grown-up Aaron to the reader
    c. Changes in Silas's and Eppie's appearances over the years
    d. Eppie's and Aaron's secret consciousness of each other

B 原文の中であなたが重要だと思ったキーワードやキーフレーズを二つ選び、それらを書き出しなさい。また、それらを選んだ理由について、それぞれ日本語で簡潔に説明しなさい。

1. キーワードやキーフレーズ (　　　　) 行目

    理由

2. キーワードやキーフレーズ (　　　　) 行目

    理由

Part 2 EXERCISES

A 以下の設問に答えなさい。

1. Which of the following statements is not true?
   a. To a great extent Silas's new self owes its origin to Eppie's arrival.
   b. Silas's love for Eppie has a lot to do with his fitting in with Raveloe life.
   c. Smoking is said to be a measure to cure Silas of his mysterious illness.
   d. Silas's obedience to Raveloe customs contributes to his physical recovery.

2. When is Silas's "best years" in line 18?
   a. Years when he believed in God and man in his youth
   b. Years when he was successful as a linen weaver
   c. Years when he brought up Eppie as a foster parent
   d. Years when he was increasingly supported by Raveloe people

3. What is not regarded as a motive that causes Silas to relate his old tale to Dolly?
   a. His realization of the link between his past and present
   b. His increasing inclination to unlock his heart to her
   c. His new habit strongly promoted by the villagers
   d. His reawakened memory of the days lost in oblivion

B 原文の中であなたが重要だと思ったキーワードやキーフレーズを二つ選び、それらを書き出しなさい。また、それらを選んだ理由について、それぞれ日本語で簡潔に説明しなさい。

1. キーワードやキーフレーズ (　　　　) 行目

   理由

2. キーワードやキーフレーズ (　　　　) 行目

   理由

Unit 9 〜 10 (原著第 14 〜 16 章) の全体のあらすじを、自分の言葉で 600 〜 800 字程度の日本語に要約しなさい。四つの英文箇所の内容に留意し、これらを適切な形で組み込むこと。

Unit 11　GodfreyとNancyの葛藤

原著第17章

> 結婚15年目を迎えたゴドフリーとナンシーの間には子供ができず、それが夫婦に微妙な影を落としていた。6年前からゴドフリーは養子を希望していた。だが、この当時は養子縁組など思いもよらぬ時代であり、自らの中で決めた規範に従う厳格な性質のナンシーは、夫の願いを受け入れなかったのだった。

Part 1

　　Godfrey had from the first specified Eppie, then about twelve years old, as a child suitable for them to adopt. It had never occurred to him that Silas would rather part with his life than with Eppie. Surely the weaver would wish the best to the child he had taken so much trouble with, and would be glad that such good fortune should
5　happen to her: she would always be very grateful to him, and he would be well provided for to the end of his life—provided for as the excellent part he had done by the child deserved. Was it not an appropriate thing for people in a higher station to take a charge off the hands of a man in a lower? It seemed an eminently appropriate thing to Godfrey, for reasons that were known only to himself; and by a common
10　fallacy, he imagined the measure would be easy because he had private motives for desiring it. This was rather a coarse mode of estimating Silas's relation to Eppie; but we must remember that many of the impressions which Godfrey was likely to gather concerning the labouring people around him would favour the idea that deep affections can hardly go along with callous palms and scant means; and he had not
15　had the opportunity, even if he had had the power, of entering intimately into all that was exceptional in the weaver's experience. It was only the want of adequate knowledge that could have made it possible for Godfrey deliberately to entertain an unfeeling project . . . .

> ゴドフリーは愛する妻の性格を知るがゆえ、エピーに関する真相を彼女に打ち明けることなど到底できなかった。彼は子宝に恵まれないのは因果応報だと思う。時が経つにつれ、妻から養子縁組を拒まれた状態では、自分の過ちを償うことはますます困難となった。

2 **would rather** 37 ページ 20 行目の注を参照。
3 **Surely the weaver would wish …** 以降は自由間接話法。40 ページのコラム 5 を参照。
4 **had taken so much trouble** 35 ページ 9 行目の注を参照。
5 **would be well provided for** provide for somebody = give somebody the things that they need to live, such as food, money and clothing (*OALD*)　e.g. He is well provided for.（彼の生活は何の不自由もない。） cf. He is ill provided for.（彼は生活に困っている。）（『ジーニアス英和大辞典』）
6 **as the excellent part … deserved** 「素晴らしい役割に相応なように、素晴らしい役割にふさわしく」
6 **the excellent part he had done by the child** do one's part = do one's duty = 「役割を果たす、本文を尽くす」　by = towards, concerning
7 **Was it not an appropriate thing for people in a higher station to take a charge off the hands of a man in a lower?** このような考え方を noblesse oblige [noublés oublí:ʒ] という。*OED* は phrase suggesting that noble ancestry constrains (to honourable behaviour); privilege entails responsibility と説明している。 station = position, rank　take a charge off … = 「…から負担（になっているもの）を取り除く」　charge = a person or thing entrusted to the care of someone　e.g. The babysitter watched over her charges.（ベビーシッターは預かった子供たちの世話をした。）（*ODE*）
10 **measure** = step, action　37 ページ 8 行目の注を参照。
10 **private** = secret
13 **favour** = support, approve
14 **go along with …** 「…に伴う、付随する」
14 **scant** = meagre, inadequate, limited　e.g. He earned a scant living as a freelance writer.（彼はフリーのライターとして細々と暮していた。）（『ジーニアス英和大辞典』）
14 **means** = financial resources, income (*ODE*)
15 **entering intimately into …** enter into … = 「…を思いやる、…を十分に理解する」
16 **want** = lack
17 **entertain** If you entertain an idea or suggestion, you allow yourself to consider it as possible or as worth thinking about seriously. (*COBUILD*)

コラム 13：　ナンシーの性質

　本書では紙面の都合上ここまでナンシーの登場場面が少なかったが、これ以降彼女はより重要な役割を担っていく。これは原著においても同様である。そこでナンシーの性質についてここで少し補足説明をしておきたい。56 ページおよび 78 ページのあらすじにあるように、彼女は愛情深いが同時に厳しい規範意識を持った貴婦人という人物造形がなされている。彼女が築き上げた内なる "unalterable little code"（不変の小さな掟）（原著第 17 章）は、夫からの養子縁組案を拒む要因となる。同章でナンシーは、"Dear Godfrey, don't ask me to do what I know is wrong: I should never be happy again. I know it's very hard for *you*—it's easier for me—but it's the will of Providence" と訴える。「間違っていると私がわかっていることをするよう言わないで」という言葉には彼女の高い倫理性や道徳意識が窺えるが、さらに重要なのは、それが「神意」と結びついている点である。これに続く箇所でエリオットは、ナンシーがその限られた狭い環境の中で、系統だった信仰心を持つ敬虔な人々が抱くような考え方に独力で辿り着いていたという驚異に言及している。この高尚な宗教性と、同じくラヴィロウ在住の女性ドリーの無教養だが素朴な信心ぶり（75 ページのコラム 12 を参照）とのコントラストに着目してみるのも、一つの有用な読み方となるだろう。

原著第18章

> ゴドフリーが真っ青な顔で帰宅する。排水工事のために石切場の水が干上がり、行方不明になっていたダンシーの遺体が発見されたのだ。そばにはサイラスの大金もあり、彼が盗んだ事実が判明した。遅かれ早かれすべては神意によって明るみに出るのだと悟ったゴドフリーは、ナンシーに対して過去の秘密を告白し始める。

Part 2

"Nancy," said Godfrey, slowly, "when I married you, I hid something from you—something I ought to have told you. That woman Marner found dead in the snow—Eppie's mother—that wretched woman—was my wife: Eppie is my child."

He paused, dreading the effect of his confession. But Nancy sat quite still, only that her eyes dropped and ceased to meet his. She was pale and quiet as a meditative statue, clasping her hands on her lap.

"You'll never think the same of me again," said Godfrey, after a little while, with some tremor in his voice.

She was silent.

"I oughtn't to have left the child unowned: I oughtn't to have kept it from you. But I couldn't bear to give you up, Nancy. I was led away into marrying her—I suffered for it."

Still Nancy was silent, looking down; and he almost expected that she would presently get up and say she would go to her father's. How could she have any mercy for faults that must seem so black to her, with her simple, severe notions?

But at last she lifted up her eyes to his again and spoke. There was no indignation in her voice—only deep regret.

"Godfrey, if you had but told me this six years ago, we could have done some of our duty by the child. Do you think I'd have refused to take her in, if I'd known she was yours?"

At that moment Godfrey felt all the bitterness of an error that was not simply futile, but had defeated its own end. He had not measured this wife with whom he had lived so long. But she spoke again, with more agitation.

"And—O, Godfrey—if we'd had her from the first, if you'd taken to her as you ought, she'd have loved me for her mother—and you'd have been happier with me: I could better have bore my little baby dying, and our life might have been more like what we used to think it 'ud be."

The tears fell, and Nancy ceased to speak.

> 震えおののきながら許しを請う夫を、ナンシーは進んで許した。ゴドフリーがエピーを引き取る意向を伝えると、ナンシーも彼女を認知して養ってやるのが彼の義務だと同意し、二人はサイラスのところへ赴くことにする。

4 **only that …** 31 ページ 15 行目の注を参照。that は省略可能。

7 **think the same of me** the same は副詞用法で in like manner の意味。

10 **unowned** = unacknowledged

10 **have kept it from you** If you keep something from someone, you do not tell them about it. (*COBUILD*)

11 **I was led away** lead away (vt.) = induce to follow unthinkingly (*OED*)

13 **How could she … ?** 自由間接話法。40 ページのコラム 5 を参照。

14 **black** = foul, iniquitous, atrocious, horribly wicked (*OED*)

17 **but** = only

18 **by** 79 ページ 6 行目の注を参照。

18 **take her in** 「引き取る」 cf. If you take someone in, you allow them to stay in your house or your country, especially when they do not have anywhere to stay or are in trouble. (*COBUILD*)

19 **was not simply futile, but had defeated …** = was not only futile, but also had defeated … defeat = frustrate, thwart

22 **if you'd taken to her** take to … = start liking … (*OALD*)

23 **for** = as 資格、特性を表す for。e.g. They chose Tom for their leader.（彼らはトムをリーダーとして選んだ。） They passed for brothers.（彼らは兄弟として通っていた。）

24 **have bore my little baby dying** = have borne the death of my little baby (研究社版注釈 332) borne= endured 14 年前にナンシーは自身が身ごもった赤ん坊を亡くしている。

25 **'ud** 35 ページ 16 行目の注を参照。

コラム 14： 偶然と因果律

　ゴドフリーの告白は、"Everything comes to light, Nancy, sooner or later. When God Almighty wills it, our secrets are found out"（原著第 18 章）という諦念から生じている。神意に言及するこの認識は、ゴドフリーがナンシーと同じく敬虔なキリスト教徒であることの証左であるが、同時に、そこには彼の内的性質およびエリオットの思想が関わっている。

　ゴドフリーの性質として顕著なのは、Unit 4 Part 2 の 20 行目や Unit 6 のあらすじに登場した、「偶然」あるいは「運」への依存である。原著では chance(s) や fortune といった語がゴドフリーの行動を巡るコメントとして頻出する。大文字で Fortune と書けばギリシャ・ローマ神話の「運命の女神」を指すが、これと同じようにエリオットは神格化された偶然を登場させ、"Favourable Chance is the god of all men who follow their own devices instead of obeying a law they believe in"（都合の良い偶然というのは、自分が信奉する掟には従わず、自らの気ままな意向に追随するあらゆる人間にとっては神なのである）（原著第 9 章）と揶揄している。この神が最初に述べたキリスト教的な神と異なるのは言うまでもない。

　偶然や運の反意語は「因果（関係）」「因果律」(cause and effect, causality, etc.) である。エリオットはそれを "the orderly sequence by which the seed brings forth a crop after its kind"（種子はその種類に応じて収穫をもたらすという秩序だった因果的連鎖）（原著第 9 章）と表現している（cf. 旧約聖書創世記第 1 章 11-12 節、新約聖書ガラテヤの信徒への手紙第 6 章 7 節）。エリオットは登場人物の行動においても作品のプロットにおいても因果律を重視する作家で、当然のことながら、偶然や運に頼り自己の責任を回避してきたゴドフリーには、後年になって相応の報いを与える。自分の家が子宝に恵まれない状況を彼は "retribution"（原著第 17 章、78 ページ下部のあらすじを参照）と認識するが、その背景にはこのような思想が存在している。本書 Introduction でも触れたように、エリオットは "The Nemesis is a very mild one" と述べているが、読者はどのように判断するだろうか。

　付言すると、ランタン・ヤードでサイラスの罪状を決定づけたくじ (lot) には「運命」という意味もあるが、これはどのように考えられるだろうか。25 ページ 15 行目の注も参照。

Part 1 EXERCISES

A 以下の設問に答えなさい。

1. What is this passage mainly about?
    a. Godfrey's reasonable exploitation of those born humble
    b. Godfrey's unsympathetic understanding of Silas and Eppie
    c. Godfrey's solid claim to distinction through his generosity
    d. Godfrey's considerate acceptance of Eppie's adoption

2. What idea does Godfrey not conceive?
    a. Silas may lack profound attachment to Eppie due to his low status.
    b. Silas deserves to be taken care of on account of his raising Eppie.
    c. Silas is to accept the offer Godfrey makes for Eppie.
    d. Silas should be rewarded regardless of Eppie's future.

2. What attitude or emotion does the author show towards Godfrey?
    a. pity and denial
    b. criticism and understanding
    c. approval and respect
    d. apprehension and disrespect

B 原文の中であなたが重要だと思ったキーワードやキーフレーズを二つ選び、それらを書き出しなさい。また、それらを選んだ理由について、それぞれ日本語で簡潔に説明しなさい。

1. キーワードやキーフレーズ (　　　　) 行目

   理由

2. キーワードやキーフレーズ (　　　　) 行目

   理由

Part 2 EXERCISES

A 以下の設問に答えなさい。

1. Which of the following statements is not true about Nancy's reactions?

    a. She keeps averting her eyes from Godfrey at first.

    b. She ends in weeping, unable to contain herself.

    c. She sits like a carved figure, lost for words.

    d. She cannot help losing her temper without delay.

2. What does Nancy think the result would have been if Godfrey had confessed earlier?

    a. The easing of pain concerning their child who passed away

    b. The unbearable undertaking of their parental obligation

    c. The realization of their past prospect of bitterness in life

    d. The reawakening of tender feelings for Nancy in the adopted child

3. What does not occur to Godfrey's mind?

    a. Fear that his past matrimony will make the present one difficult

    b. Conviction that what he risks will deliver him from his hardship

    c. Apprehension that Nancy's severity will urge her to desert him

    d. Criticism that he has put off the chance of undelayed confession

B 原文の中であなたが重要だと思ったキーワードやキーフレーズを二つ選び、それらを書き出しなさい。また、それらを選んだ理由について、それぞれ日本語で簡潔に説明しなさい。

1. キーワードやキーフレーズ (　　　　) 行目

   理由

2. キーワードやキーフレーズ (　　　　) 行目

   理由

Unit 12　Silas と Eppie の絆

原著第 19 章

　ゴドフリーがナンシーに秘密を告白した同じ日の夜、サイラスとエピーは戻ってきた金貨の山を前にして座っていた。サイラスはエピーのことが最も大切であり、今となっては金が自分の心を奪うことはないと話した。そこへゴドフリーとナンシーがやってくる。ゴドフリーはダンシーの件を詫びた後、サイラスの老齢について触れつつ、慎重にエピー引き取りの話題を切り出した。サイラスの心は動揺する。エピーは感謝の意を表しつつも、丁寧にゴドフリーの申し出を断った。ゴドフリーは思わずかっとなって言葉を発した。

Part 1

　"But I've a claim on you, Eppie—the strongest of all claims. It's my duty, Marner, to own Eppie as my child, and provide for her. She is my own child: her mother was my wife. I've a natural claim on her that must stand before every other."

　Eppie had given a violent start, and turned quite pale. Silas, on the contrary, who had been relieved, by Eppie's answer, from the dread lest his mind should be in opposition to hers, felt the spirit of resistance in him set free, not without a touch of parental fierceness. "Then, sir," he answered, with an accent of bitterness that had been silent in him since the memorable day when his youthful hope had perished—"then, sir, why didn't you say so sixteen year ago, and claim her before I'd come to love her, i'stead o' coming to take her from me now, when you might as well take the heart out o' my body? God gave her to me because you turned your back upon her, and He looks upon her as mine: you've no right to her! When a man turns a blessing from his door, it falls to them as take it in."

　"I know that, Marner. I was wrong. I've repented of my conduct in that matter," said Godfrey, who could not help feeling the edge of Silas's words.

　"I'm glad to hear it, sir," said Marner, with gathering excitement; "but repentance doesn't alter what's been going on for sixteen year. Your coming now and saying "I'm her father" doesn't alter the feelings inside us. It's me she's been calling her father ever since she could say the word."

　"But I think you might look at the thing more reasonably, Marner," said Godfrey, unexpectedly awed by the weaver's direct truth-speaking. "It isn't as if she was to be taken quite away from you, so that you'd never see her again. She'll be very near you, and come to see you very often. She'll feel just the same towards you."

　"Just the same?" said Marner, more bitterly than ever. "How'll she feel just the same for me as she does now, when we eat o' the same bit, and drink o' the same cup, and think o' the same things from one day's end to another? Just the same? that's idle talk. You'd cut us i' two."

2 **provide for ...**　79 ページ 5 行目の注を参照。
3 **stand before ...** = be more important than ... , be in preference to ...　e.g. John stands before all the other students in mathematics.（ジョンは数学に関して他のどの生徒よりも優れている。）（『ジーニアス英和大辞典』）31 ページ 19 行目の注を参照
4 **start** = a sudden movement of surprise or alarm (*ODE*)　動詞の start については、67 ページ 6 行目の注を参照。
5 **lest ...**　通常は動詞や動詞句の後に用いるが、ここでは直前の名詞 dread の後に続いて、その内容を表している。
6 **set free** = liberated (p.p.)
7 **accent** = tone, manner of speaking
9 **sixteen year ago** = sixteen years ago　year は俗語方言に残っている古い複数形。16 行目の year も同様。(研究社版注釈 336)
9 **i'stead o'** = instead of　i' については 45 ページ 15 行目、o' については 35 ページ 19 行目の注を参照。次行 (10 行目) の out o' の o'、24〜25 行目の o' the same の o'、26 行目の i' two の i' も同様の脱落。
10 **you might as well ...**　you might as well ... (as 〜) =「（〜するのは）…するのと同じだ、（〜するくらいなら）…した方がましだ」省略されている as 〜を補うとすれば、as take her from me。e.g. You might as well give up the project as do it incompletely.（計画を中途半端にやるというのは、やめてしまうのと同じだ。）（『ロイヤル英文法』441）
11 **you turned your back upon her**　turn one's back (up)on ... = reject or abandon (a person or thing that one was previously involved with) (*ODE*)
12 **falls to ...**　fall = come as a lot, portion, or possession (*OED*)　e.g. The estate fell to my cousin.（その屋敷は私のいとこのものとなった。）
12 **them as ...** = those who ...（『方言研究』670）45 ページ 12 行目の注を参照。
12 **take it in**　81 ページ 18 行目の注を参照。
14 **edge** = keenness, effectiveness, force
15 **gathering** = intensifying, increasing
17 **It's me she's been calling her father** = It's me that she has been calling her father
19 **you might ...**　依頼や軽い命令を表す might。e.g. You might (= I request you to) post this for me.（これをポストに入れておいてくれたまえ。）（『リーダーズ英和辞典』）
20 **It isn't as if ...**　e.g. Look, what's the problem here? It isn't as if I committed a crime!（いいかい、どこに問題があるんだ。わたしが罪を犯したというわけでもないのに。）（『ジーニアス英和大辞典』）
24 **when we eat o' the same bit ...**　旧約聖書のサムエル記下第 12 章 3 節にある以下の内容を踏まえた表現。But the poor *man* had nothing, save one little ewe lamb, which he had bought and nourished up: and it grew up together with him, and with his children; it did eat of his own meat, and drank of his own cup, and lay in his bosom, and was unto him as a daughter.（貧しい男は自分で買った一匹の雌の小羊のほかに／何一つ持っていなかった。彼はその小羊を養い／小羊は彼のもとで育ち、息子たちと一緒にいて／彼の皿から食べ、彼の椀から飲み／彼のふところで眠り、彼にとっては娘のようだった。）(Penguin 版注釈 193; 研究社版注釈 336)
25 **from one day's end to another**　cf. from one year's end to another [the other] =「毎年毎年、長年の間」(『研究社新英和大辞典』)
26 **idle** = without purpose or effect; pointless　e.g. He did not want to waste valuable time in idle chatter.（彼は貴重な時間を無意味なおしゃべりで無駄にしたくなかった。）(*ODE*)

> ゴドフリーは、頑なな態度を取るサイラスのことを、娘の幸福を考えぬ利己的な人間だと思い、繰り返し自分の義務と権利を主張した。ナンシーも、持ち前の厳しい規範により、育ての親より血のつながった親に権利があると考えていた。サイラスはエピーの判断にすべてを委ねることにする。エピーはサイラスの手を握りしめ、これまでよりも冷静な決意で話し出した

Part 2

"Thank you, ma'am—thank you, sir, for your offers—they're very great, and far above my wish. For I should have no delight i' life any more if I was forced to go away from my father, and knew he was sitting at home, a-thinking of me and feeling lone. We've been used to be happy together every day, and I can't think o' no happiness without him. And he says he'd nobody i' the world till I was sent to him, and he'd have nothing when I was gone. And he's took care of me and loved me from the first, and I'll cleave to him as long as he lives, and nobody shall ever come between him and me."

"But you must make sure, Eppie," said Silas, in a low voice—"you must make sure as you won't ever be sorry, because you've made your choice to stay among poor folks, and with poor clothes and things, when you might ha' had everything o' the best."

His sensitiveness on this point had increased as he listened to Eppie's words of faithful affection.

"I can never be sorry, father," said Eppie. "I shouldn't know what to think on or to wish for with fine things about me, as I haven't been used to. And it 'ud be poor work for me to put on things, and ride in a gig, and sit in a place at church, as 'ud make them as I'm fond of think me unfitting company for 'em. What could *I* care for then?"

Nancy looked at Godfrey with a pained questioning glance. But his eyes were fixed on the floor, where he was moving the end of his stick, as if he were pondering on something absently. She thought there was a word which might perhaps come better from her lips than from his.

"What you say is natural, my dear child—it's natural you should cling to those who've brought you up," she said, mildly; "but there's a duty you owe to your lawful father. There's perhaps something to be given up on more sides than one. When your father opens his home to you, I think it's right you shouldn't turn your back on it."

"I can't feel as I've got any father but one," said Eppie, impetuously, while the tears gathered. "I've always thought of a little home where he'd sit i' the corner, and I should fend and do everything for him: I can't think o' no other home. I wasn't brought up to be a lady, and I can't turn my mind to it. I like the working-folks, and their victuals, and their ways. And," she ended passionately, while the tears fell, "I'm promised to marry a working-man, as'll live with father, and help me to take care of him."

1 **ma'am** = a colloquial shortening of madam   Formerly the ordinary respectful form of address to a woman (originally only to a married woman) of equal or superior rank or station (*OED*)
2 **should**   35ページ18行目の注を参照。14行目の shouldn't も同様。
2 **i'** = in   45ページ15行目の注を参照。5行目と27行目も同様。
3 **a-thinking**   45ページ13行目の注を参照。
4 **I can't think o' no happiness** = I can't think of any happiness   二重否定の形になっているが、意味としては全否定。このような表現は、非標準的な俗語体あるいは無教育な者の話し方とされる。28行目も同様。
5 **he'd nobody** = he had nobody
6 **he'd have nothing** = he would have nothing
6 **he's took care** = he's taken care
7 **shall**   51ページ15行目の注を参照。
9 **make sure** = check, confirm
10 **as** = that（接続詞） 26行目も同様。45ページ12行目の注を参照。
10 **sorry** = repentant, penitent
11 **things** = clothes or possessions (*COBUILD*)   これらの意味の場合、複数形で用いられる。
11 **when you might ha' had …**   when = although   e.g. Why did he give up trying, when he might have succeeded?（彼は成功したかもしれないのにどうしてあきらめてしまったのか。）（『ジーニアス英和大辞典』）ha' については55ページ9行目の注を参照。
14 **think on** = think of   of の代わりに on が用いられる方言の例。（『方言研究』240-42）
15 **as** = which（関係代名詞） 45ページ12行目の注を参照。
15 **'ud**   35ページ16行目の注を参照。
15 **poor work**   poor = insignificant, paltry   work は形容詞に修飾されて「…なやり方、行為」の意味になる。e.g. sharp work =「抜け目ないやり方」
16 **a place** = a family pew「（教会にある、仕切られた）家族専用席」cf. The space which one person occupies by usage, allotment, or right (*OED*)
16 **as 'ud make them as I'm fond of think …** = which would make those whom I'm fond of think …
17 **company** = the person or persons with whom one voluntarily or habitually associates   cf. good company, bad company, and the like, are said of one or more persons with reference to their companionable qualities (*OED*)
17 **'em** = them   ただし、これは them から [ð] 音の脱落によって生じたものではなく、中期英語 (Middle English) の hem(=them) から [h] 音が脱落したものである。（『方言研究』162, 202-03）
24 **There's perhaps something to be given up on more sides than one.** = Perhaps you are not the only one called upon to make a sacrifice.（研究社版注釈338）
25 **turn your back on it**   85ページ11行目の注を参照。
26 **but** = except
29 **victuals**   victual [vítl]
30 **I'm promised** = I've promised
31 **as** = who（関係代名詞） 45ページ12行目の注を参照。

Part 1 EXERCISES

A 以下の設問に答えなさい。

1. Which of the following statements is true?
    a. Godfrey has no retort towards Silas except his identity as Eppie's real father.
    b. This is the first time that Silas has ever let his bitter feelings show before others.
    c. Godfrey's repentant reflection on his past does not have a positive impact on Silas.
    d. Silas feels himself safe before hearing Eppie's answer which suits his convenience.

2. How does Silas react to Godfrey?
    a. He disagrees with Godfrey's hope concerning Eppie's changeable mind.
    b. He makes reference to divinity as a ground for his own assertion.
    c. He indirectly insists on the unreliability of Godfrey's blood relationship.
    d. He blames Godfrey for trying to make up for his present refusal to claim Eppie.

3. What is this passage mainly about?
    a. Godfrey's insistent claim on his legitimate fatherhood
    b. The argument that lays bare the two men's incompatibility
    c. Silas's self-denial with little regard for the consequences
    d. The discourse in which the two men decide on Eppie's right to choose

B 原文の中であなたが重要だと思ったキーワードやキーフレーズを二つ選び、それらを書き出しなさい。また、それらを選んだ理由について、それぞれ日本語で簡潔に説明しなさい。

1. キーワードやキーフレーズ (　　　　) 行目

   理由

2. キーワードやキーフレーズ (　　　　) 行目

   理由

Part 2 EXERCISES

A 以下の設問に答えなさい。

1. What does Eppie think is necessary in the years to come?
    a. A lawful parent
    b. Labourers' lifestyle
    c. A place at church
    d. Ladylike manners

2. What is not true about Eppie?
    a. Her priority is placed on the life she has led rather than that offered by Godfrey.
    b. She is so confident in her own decision as to turn down Nancy's suggestion.
    c. Her marriage has much less to do with Silas's welfare than with her own.
    d. She expects her friends to feel her new respectable conditions out of place.

3. Which of the following statements is true about a home?
    a. Eppie feels like owning a home far removed from the outside world.
    b. Nancy believes a father by blood must provide a home by all means.
    c. Nancy's tendency to stress ties of blood influences her idea of a home.
    d. Eppie's ideal of a home is derived from her anxiety about marriage.

B 原文の中であなたが重要だと思ったキーワードやキーフレーズを二つ選び、それらを書き出しなさい。また、それらを選んだ理由について、それぞれ日本語で簡潔に説明しなさい。

1. キーワードやキーフレーズ (　　　　) 行目

   理由

2. キーワードやキーフレーズ (　　　　) 行目

   理由

Unit 13 それぞれの行く末

原著第20章

> サイラスの小屋を後にしたゴドフリーとナンシーは、無言のまま帰宅した。二人は寄り添い、サイラスとエピーの言い分はもっともなこと、子供のことはすべて諦め、エピーの秘密は他言しないことを確認し合うのだった。

Part 1

Godfrey fell into thoughtfulness again. Presently he looked up at Nancy sorrowfully, and said—

"She's a very pretty, nice girl, isn't she, Nancy?"

"Yes, dear; and with just your hair and eyes: I wondered it had never struck me before."

"I think she took a dislike to me at the thought of my being her father: I could see a change in her manner after that."

"She couldn't bear to think of not looking on Marner as her father," said Nancy, not wishing to confirm her husband's painful impression.

"She thinks I did wrong by her mother as well as by her. She thinks me worse than I am. But she *must* think it: she can never know all. It's part of my punishment, Nancy, for my daughter to dislike me. I should never have got into that trouble if I'd been true to you—if I hadn't been a fool. I'd no right to expect anything but evil could come of that marriage—and when I shirked doing a father's part too."

Nancy was silent: her spirit of rectitude would not let her try to soften the edge of what she felt to be a just compunction. He spoke again after a little while, but the tone was rather changed: there was tenderness mingled with the previous self-reproach.

"And I got *you*, Nancy, in spite of all; and yet I've been grumbling and uneasy because I hadn't something else—as if I deserved it."

"You've never been wanting to me, Godfrey," said Nancy, with quiet sincerity. "My only trouble would be gone if you resigned yourself to the lot that's been given us."

"Well, perhaps it isn't too late to mend a bit there. Though it *is* too late to mend some things, say what they will."

- 4 **with just your hair and eyes** = with the hair and eyes just like yours　cf. 61 ページ 15 行目の fair に関する注を参照。
- 4 **had ... struck me**　If an idea or thought strikes you, it suddenly comes into your mind.　e.g. At this point, it suddenly struck me that I was wasting my time.（この時点で、私は自分が時間を無駄にしていると突然気づいた。）(*COBUILD*)
- 6 **took a dislike to ...**　take a dislike to ... = come to dislike ...
- 10 **by**　79 ページ 6 行目の注を参照。
- 13 **I'd no right to expect anything but evil ...**　否定語＋ anything but ... = nothing but ...　e.g. His behaviour did not bring anything but trouble. = His behaviour brought nothing but trouble.（彼の振る舞いは面倒以外何ももたらさなかった。彼の振る舞いによって面倒が生じただけだった。）25 ページ 8 行目の注も参照。
- 14 **shirked**　shirk = avoid or neglect (a duty or responsibility) (*ODE*)
- 15 **rectitude**　Rectitude is a quality or attitude that is shown by people who behave honestly and morally according to accepted standards. (*COBUILD*)　79 ページのコラム 13 も参照。
- 15 **would not**　過去の強い意志を表す would の用法。ここでは否定形で、過去の強い拒絶を表す。e.g. The rusty screw wouldn't come loose.（さびついたねじはどうしてもゆるまなかった。）(『ロイヤル英文法』452)
- 15 **edge**　85 ページ 14 行目の注を参照。
- 20 **hadn't ...** = did not have ...
- 21 **wanting** = lacking in a required or necessary quality (*ODE*)　e.g. Some people are wanting in courtesy.（礼儀に欠けている人がいる。）(『ジーニアス英和大辞典』) 79 ページ 16 行目の注も参照。
- 22 **resigned yourself to ...**　resign oneself to ... = accept something unpleasant that cannot be changed or avoided (*OALD*)
- 23 **it isn't too late to mend ...**　cf. It is never too late to mend.（(ことわざ) 行ないを改めるのに遅すぎることはない。）(『ジーニアス英和大辞典』)
- 24 **say what they will**　「人が何と言おうとも」 e.g. Say what you will, I still think she was right.（君が何と言おうとも、私はやはり彼女が正しかったと思う。）(『研究社新英和大辞典』)

（あらすじの続き）

▼**原著第 21 章**▼

> 以前から生まれ故郷のランタン・ヤード行きを考えていたサイラスは、エピーを伴って出立する。30 年ぶりに訪れた故郷は大きな工場町へと変貌していた。さらに驚いたことに、ランタン・ヤードは跡形もなくなっていた。ラヴィロウに戻ったサイラスは、このことをドリーに話す。ドリーは、わけはわからないがこれは天の神様の思し召しであり、正しい道理というものは存在するのだと答えた。サイラスは、エピーが授けられて以来自分は信ずる光を得たのであり、彼女が決してそばを離れないと言うのだから、死ぬまで信じていこうと思うと話すのだった。

原著最終章

Part 2

There was one time of the year which was held in Raveloe to be especially suitable for a wedding. It was when the great lilacs and laburnums in the old-fashioned gardens showed their golden and purple wealth above the lichen-tinted walls, and when there were calves still young enough to want bucketfuls of fragrant milk. People were not so busy then as they must become when the full cheese-making and the mowing had set in; and besides, it was a time when a light bridal dress could be worn with comfort and seen to advantage.

Happily the sunshine fell more warmly than usual on the lilac tufts the morning that Eppie was married, for her dress was a very light one. She had often thought, though with a feeling of renunciation, that the perfection of a wedding-dress would be a white cotton, with the tiniest pink sprig at wide intervals; so that when Mrs Godfrey Cass begged to provide one, and asked Eppie to choose what it should be, previous meditation had enabled her to give a decided answer at once.

Seen at a little distance as she walked across the churchyard and down the village, she seemed to be attired in pure white, and her hair looked like the dash of gold on a lily. One hand was on her husband's arm, and with the other she clasped the hand of her father Silas.

"You won't be giving me away, father," she had said before they went to church; "you'll only be taking Aaron to be a son to you."

Dolly Winthrop walked behind with her husband; and there ended the little bridal procession.

> 多くの人々がこの婚礼の行列を眺めていた。赤屋敷では、所用で不在のゴドフリーを除いた面々が一行を祝福した。虹亭では、身寄りのない子供を父親代わりになって育てたことでサイラスは天啓を授かったのだ、という考えで全員が一致した。ドリーの夫は虹亭で皆から祝福を受けることとなり、あとの一行はサイラスの家へと向かうのだった。

Eppie had a larger garden than she had ever expected there now; and in other ways there had been alterations at the expense of Mr Cass, the landlord, to suit Silas's larger family. For he and Eppie had declared that they would rather stay at the Stone-pits than go to any new home. The garden was fenced with stones on two sides, but in front there was an open fence, through which the flowers shone with answering gladness, as the four united people came within sight of them.

"O father," said Eppie, "what a pretty home ours is! I think nobody could be happier than we are."

1 **held**　23 ページ 14 行目の注を参照。
3 **wealth** = abundance
3 **lichen** [láikən]
4 **calves** [ká:vz] = plural form of calf [ká:f]
6 **had set in** = had begun
7 **to advantage** = so as to increase or augment the effect of anything; advantageously, favourably (*OED*)　e.g. The photo showed his figure to advantage.（その写真は彼の姿を引き立たせた。）
10 **the perfection of a wedding-dress**　The perfection of something such as a skill, system, or product involves making it as good as it could possibly be. (*COBUILD*)　e.g. The former prime minister was generally considered as the perfection of a corrupt political system.（前の首相は腐敗した政治体制の極致だと一般に考えられていた。）
11 **so that**　31 ページ 18 行目の注を参照。
15 **dash** = a small portion (of colour, etc.) as it were dashed or thrown carelessly upon a surface (*OED*)
18 **You won't be giving me away**　In a Christian wedding ceremony, if someone gives the bride away, they officially present her to her husband. This is traditionally done by the bride's father. (*COBUILD*)
24 **would rather**　37 ページ 20 行目の注を参照。
27 **answering**　73 ページ 3 行目の注を参照。

Part 1 EXERCISES

A 以下の設問に答えなさい。

1. Which of the following statements is true?
    a. Nancy gives her full consent to Godfrey's emotional appeal.
    b. Godfrey's submission to the destiny is hardly what Nancy expects.
    c. What Godfrey finally attains is the recognition of Nancy's worth.
    d. Nancy has noticed resemblances between Eppie and Godfrey before.

2. What does Godfrey think is included in the reasons for Eppie's distant air?
    a. Eppie's ill-mannered approach to her father
    b. Godfrey's ill-treatment of his present wife
    c. Eppie's ill-feeling towards Godfrey's fatherhood
    d. Godfrey's ill-timed disclosure of his achievement

3. What can be included in "some things" in the last line?
    a. Godfrey's concern about his childless condition
    b. Godfrey's actual indiscretion in the past
    c. Godfrey's discontent, causing Nancy worry
    d. Godfrey's reluctance to accept the fate

B 原文の中であなたが重要だと思ったキーワードやキーフレーズを二つ選び、それらを書き出しなさい。また、それらを選んだ理由について、それぞれ日本語で簡潔に説明しなさい。

1. キーワードやキーフレーズ (　　　　) 行目

　　理由

2. キーワードやキーフレーズ (　　　　) 行目

　　理由

Part 2 EXERCISES

A　以下の設問に答えなさい。

1. What is the season considered to be when this episode takes place?
   a. late winter or early spring
   b. late spring or early summer
   c. late summer or early autumn
   d. late autumn or early winter

2. Which of the following statements is not true as an explanation of this season?
   a. People tend to lead a life of leisure.
   b. The season makes brides more pleasing in appearance.
   c. Flowers typical of the season are in bloom.
   d. There is no shortage of milk provided by young cows.

3. What is true about Eppie?
   a. She feels grateful as her wish to move out is favorably answered by Silas.
   b. Having giving up on a wedding dress, she finds Nancy's offer agreeable.
   c. Her appropriate choice of a wedding dress helps her mix in with fashionable society.
   d. Her living conditions have improved owing to her demands on Godfrey.

B　原文の中であなたが重要だと思ったキーワードやキーフレーズを二つ選び、それらを書き出しなさい。また、それらを選んだ理由について、それぞれ日本語で簡潔に説明しなさい。

1.　キーワードやキーフレーズ（　　　　　）行目

　　理由

2.　キーワードやキーフレーズ（　　　　　）行目

　　理由

Unit 11 ～ 13（原著第17章～最終章）の全体のあらすじを、自分の言葉で 600 ～ 800 字程度の日本語に要約しなさい。六つの英文箇所の内容に留意し、これらを適切な形で組み込むこと。

Unit 14　レポートを書こう

　これまで読んできた『サイラス・マーナー』の作品内容をもとに、レポートを作成してみよう。論述式のレポートは読書感想文やあらすじ紹介とは異なる。作品を客観的に分析し、独自のテーマ（主題）を立て、論を展開し、一定の結論を導き出すことが求められる。学期末のレポートであれば、たとえば原稿用紙で5枚から10枚ほどのものもあろうし、また、日本語で書く場合も英語で書く場合もあるだろう。以降の説明は、標準的な長さの学期末レポートを日本語で執筆することを想定している。もちろん、レポート作成の手順に関してはいろいろな考え方があるだろう。以下のやり方はその一例であるということを最初にお断りしておきたい。

　レポート執筆で重要なのはテーマの設定である。そのための足掛かりとして、すでに皆さんは、各Unitの各Partにおいて、自分が重要だと思うキーワードやキーフレーズを選び出す作業を行ってきた。もちろん、最初のうちはテーマを見つけるという明確な意図ではなく、各Partを読んだ際の素朴な反応に基づいてそれらを選んだことだろう。その感性はぜひ大事にしてもらいたい。だが同時に、作品を読み進めるにつれ、自分が何らかの判断基準に基づいて、あるいは作品中で特徴的に、時には反復して用いられる表現や象徴性などに着目しながら、関連性のある語群を選んでいたのではないだろうか。また、各キーワードやキーフレーズを選ぶ際にはその理由についても書き留めてきたが、そこには何かしらの共通項や方向性が表れていないだろうか。それらはテーマ設定へ向けての大きな要素となり、また、後に論を支える具体的な材料となる。通常、レポートを書くためにはいろいろなメモを取る必要があるが、皆さんはその最初の段階のプロセスをPartごとに実践してきたわけである。

　では、以下の手順にそってレポート作成に取り組んでみよう。これらは実際の原稿執筆に至る前までの段階的な準備のプロセスである。

1. 最初に、これまで選んだ多くのキーワードやキーフレーズの中から、互いに関連性を持つと思われるものを自分なりに厳選し、さらに5〜10個程度に絞り込んで簡潔に書き出してみよう。その際、それらを選んだ理由を記した箇所もあわせて読み直そう。さらに言えば、作品を読了した現時点で改めて各Partを読み直すことで、新たな重要表現を発見することができるかもしれない。時間が許すならトライしてほしいが、その判断は皆さんに委ねたい。

2. 次に、上記キーワードやキーフレーズをもとにし、それらから集約されるテーマを暫定的に一つ書き出してみよう。このテーマは最終的にレポートの題名につながることが期待される。よって、日本語で明確かつ具体的に表現することが望ましい。必要に応じて、そのテーマにキーワードやキーフレーズ中の英語、あるいはその和訳を一部含めても良い。なお、この段階でテーマを一つに決められない場合は複数書いてもかまわないが、最終的には一つに絞って確定する必要がある。

3. 上記テーマ（複数ある場合はどれか一つ）を念頭に、1.のキーワードやキーフレーズが相互にどう関連しているかを図式化し、自分の書きたい内容を視覚的に把握、整理してみよう。順番を入れ替えたり、カテゴリー分けや階層化をしたり、矢印や囲みを用いて相関図やフローチャートを作ったり、自由な発想とやり方で行ってもらいたい。もちろん、キーワードやキーフレーズばかりでなく、それらを補う言葉や、互いの関係を説明する言葉などを、日本語でも英語でも適宜自在に入れてかまわない。逆に、1.に記したキーワードやキーフレーズをすべて用いて書く必要はないかもしれない。テーマにそって取捨選択するプロセスは当然起こりうる。

4. 上記の作業をもとに、改めてレポートのテーマを定めよう。結果的に 2. と同じものになっても良いが、この段階では確固たるテーマを決定したい。2. に記したように、このテーマはレポートの題名につながるものとなる。

5. テーマが確定したら、それに基づいて、全体的な論旨を簡潔に一文(one sentence)でまとめてみよう。これは thesis statement と言われるもので、自分が提起したテーマに対する解答までを含むものとなる。これにより、結論を見据えた形で、論の内容や方向性をさらに明確にすることが可能となる。長さは一行でも数行にわたっても良いが、一文で書くことが望ましい。具体的には、ここでは「…に関して」という抽象的な書き方ではなく、文章として叙述的に書き、最後をたとえば「…である」「…を表している」といったようにあえて断定的に言い切ってもらいたい。これにより、主張したい論旨と結論を自らに明示する。

6. 上記 thesis statement に基づいて、具体的なアウトラインを箇条書き形式で書いてみよう。まず最初にテーマを明記した簡潔な導入（introduction）、続いて本論（body）、最後に結論（conclusion）を置く。本論はさらに細分化した複数の項目からなる。項目の数は人によって異なるだろうが、あまり多いと論が散漫になる可能性があるので注意したい。大事なのは、結論に向けて、不要な脱線をすることなく、論の一貫性を意識しながら体系的に項目を立てていくことである。

・導入

・本論

項目数は各自で考える
{
  ・
  ・
  ・
}

・結論

7. 基本的なアウトラインができたら、それをさらに肉付けしよう。本論の各項目で書くべき内容をさらに具体化していく作業である。その際に重要となるのは、やはり作品をしっかり読み返し、さらに、自説を立証するために必要な引用箇所を適切に選ぶことである。レポートの内容をより確かなものにしてくれるのは、何より作品原典なのである。この作業のために、1. で選んだキーワードやキーフレーズが再度役立つことは言うまでもない。

8. ここまでの準備ができたら、いよいよ原稿執筆に移ろう。実際に書いてみると、これまでのプロセスの重要さが実感できると思うが、その一方で想定通りには進まない部分もいくらか出てくるかもしれない。その際には、これまでの作成手順を適宜見返し、不都合な箇所は必要に応じて修正することにより、レポートを完成に近づけてもらいたい。いったん書き上げた後は、提出の前に、時間をかけて推敲作業を行うことを忘れないようにしよう。

9. 最後に、具体的な執筆要領（原稿のサイズや枚数、全体の文字数、フォントの種類やサイズなどの諸フォーマット）、作品からの引用の仕方、盗用（plagiarism）に関する注意事項、パソコン使用上の留意点、データのバックアップ方法その他については、授業担当教員の指導に従ってもらいたい。

付録

『サイラス・マーナー』やジョージ・エリオットについてさらに発展的に学びたいという学習者のために、以下に参考文献リストを記載する。今後、たとえば卒業論文などで本格的に取り組む機会があれば利用していただきたい。もちろん、学期末レポートの作成においても役立ててもらえれば幸いである。

SELECTED BIBLIOGRAPHY

<エリオットの書簡・評論>

Ashton, Rosemary, ed. *George Eliot: Selected Critical Writings*. Oxford: Oxford UP, 1992.
Byatt, A. S., and Nicholas Warren, eds. *George Eliot: Selected Essays, Poems and Other Writings*. Harmondsworth: Penguin, 1990.
Haight, Gordon S., ed. *The George Eliot Letters*. 9 vols. New Haven: Yale UP, 1954-78.
Pinney, Thomas, ed. *Essays of George Eliot*. London: Routledge, 1963.
川本静子, 原公章編訳『ジョージ・エリオット 評論と書評』彩流社, 2010.

<手引・概説>

Levine, George, ed. *The Cambridge Companion to George Eliot*. Cambridge: Cambridge UP, 2001.
Rignall, John, ed. *Oxford Reader's Companion to George Eliot*. Oxford: Oxford UP, 2000.
内田能嗣, 原公章編著『あらすじで読むジョージ・エリオットの小説』大阪教育図書, 2010.

<伝記>

Ashton, Rosemary. *George Eliot: A Life*. London: Hamish Hamilton, 1996.
Bodenheimer, Rosemarie. *The Real Life of Mary Ann Evans: George Eliot, Her Letters and Fiction*. Ithaca: Cornell UP, 1994.
Cross, John Walter. *George Eliot's Life as Related in Her Letters and Journals*. 3 vols. Edinburgh: Blackwood, 1885.
Haight, Gordon S. *George Eliot: A Biography*. Oxford: Oxford UP, 1968. Harmondsworth: Penguin, 1985.

<研究書>

Allen, Walter. *George Eliot*. New York: Macmillan, 1964.
Ashton, Rosemary. *George Eliot*. Oxford: Oxford UP, 1983.『ジョージ・エリオット』前田絢子訳 雄松堂, 1988.
Auster, Henry. *Local Habitations: Regionalism in the Early Novels of George Eliot*. Cambridge, MA: Harvard UP, 1970.
Bennett, Joan. *George Eliot: Her Mind and Her Art*. Cambridge: Cambridge UP, 1948.
Carroll, David, ed. *George Eliot: The Critical Heritage*. London: Routledge, 1971.
Creeger, George R., ed. *George Eliot: A Collection of Critical Essays*. Englewood Cliffs: Prentice-Hall, 1970.
Dolin, Tim. *George Eliot*. Authors in Context. Oxford: Oxford UP, 2005.『ジョージ・エリオット』廣野由美子訳　時代のなかの作家たち5　彩流社, 2013.
Draper, R. P., ed. *George Eliot: The Mill on the Floss and Silas Marner: A Casebook*. Basingstoke: Macmillan, 1977.
Goodman, Barbara A., ed. *Readings on Silas Marner*. San Diego: Greenhaven, 2000.
Hardy, Barbara. *The Novels of George Eliot: A Study in Form*. London: Athlone, 1959.

Henry, Nancy. *The Cambridge Introduction to George Eliot*. Cambridge: Cambridge UP, 2008. 『評伝——ジョージ・エリオット』内田能嗣，小野ゆき子，会田瑞枝訳　英宝社, 2014.

Knoepflmacher, U. C. *George Eliot's Early Novels: The Limits of Realism*. Berkeley: U of California P, 1968.

Leavis, F. R. *The Great Tradition*. London: Chatto, 1948.『偉大な伝統』長岩寛，田中純蔵訳　英潮社, 1972.

Paris, Bernard J. *Experiments in Life: George Eliot's Quest for Values*. Detroit: Wayne State UP, 1965.

Pinion, F. B. *A George Eliot Companion: Literary Achievement and Modern Significance*. London: Macmillan, 1981.

Pool, Daniel. *What Jane Austen Ate and Charles Dickens Knew: From Fox Hunting to Whist—the Facts of Daily Life in Nineteenth-Century England*. New York: Simon, 1993.『19世紀のロンドンはどんな匂いがしたのだろう』片岡信訳　青土社, 1997.

Squires, Michael. *The Pastoral Novel: Studies in George Eliot, Thomas Hardy, and D. H. Lawrence*. Charlottesville: UP of Virginia, 1974.

Swinden, Patrick. *Silas Marner: Memory and Salvation*. New York: Twayne, 1992.

Thale, Jerome. *The Novels of George Eliot*. New York: Columbia UP, 1959.

Uglow, Jennifer. *George Eliot*. London: Virago, 1987.

Willey, Basil. *Nineteenth Century Studies: Coleridge to Matthew Arnold*. London: Chatto, 1949. 『十九世紀イギリス思想』米田一彦他訳　みすず書房, 1985.

天野みゆき『ジョージ・エリオットと言語・イメージ・対話』南雲堂, 2004.

海老根宏，内田能嗣共編著『ジョージ・エリオットの時空——小説の再評価』北星堂, 2000.

川本静子『ジョージ・エリオット　他者との絆を求めて』冬樹社, 1980.

<論文>

Carroll, David. "*Silas Marner*: Reversing the Oracles of Religion." *Literary Monographs*. Ed. Eric Rothstein and Thomas K. Dunseath. Vol. 1. Madison: U of Wisconsin P, 1967. 165-200.

Cohen, Susan, R. "A History and a Metamorphosis: Continuity and Discontinuity in *Silas Marner*." *Texas Studies in Literature and Language* 25 (1983): 410-26.

Dunham, Robert H. "*Silas Marner* and the Wordsworthian Child." *Studies in English Literature 1500-1900* 16 (1976): 645-59.

Fisch, Harold. "Biblical Realism in *Silas Marner*." *Identity and Ethos*. Ed. Mark H. Gelber. New York: Peter Lang, 1986. 343-60.

Gilbert, Sandra M. "Life's Empty Pack: Notes towards a Literary Daughteronomy." *Critical Inquiry* 11 (1985): 355-84.

Hawes, Donald. "Chance in *Silas Marner*." *English* 31 (1982): 213-18.

Leavis, Q. D. Introduction. *Silas Marner*. By George Eliot. Harmondsworth: Penguin, 1967. 7-43.

McLaverty, James. "Comtean Fetishism in *Silas Marner*." *Nineteenth-Century Fiction* 36 (1981): 318-36.

Shuttleworth, Sally. "Fairy Tale or Science? Physiological Psychology in *Silas Marner*." *Languages of Nature: Critical Essays on Science and Literature*. Ed. L. J. Jordanova. London: Free Assn., 1986. 244-88.

Simpson, Peter. "Crisis and Recovery: William Wordsworth, George Eliot, and *Silas Marner*." *U of Toronto Quarterly* 48 (1979): 95-114.

Swann, Brian. "*Silas Marner* and the New Mythus." *Criticism* 18 (1976): 101-21.

Thomson, Fred C. "The Theme of Alienation in *Silas Marner*." *Nineteenth-Century Fiction* 20 (1965): 69-84.

George Eliot
Silas Marner: The Weaver of Raveloe
(日本ジョージ・エリオット協会 20 周年記念企画)

2017 年 12 月 1 日 初版第 1 刷発行

監　修　日本ジョージ・エリオット協会
編注者　池園　宏・西山　史子・藤原　知予
発行者　横山　哲彌
印刷所　岩岡印刷株式会社

発行所　大阪教育図書株式会社
　　　　〒530-0055　大阪市北区野崎町 1-25
　　　　TEL 06-6361-5936　　FAX 06-6361-5819
　　　　振替　00940-1-115500

ISBN978-4-271-41023-2　C3087　　落丁・乱丁本はお取り替え致します。
本書のコピー、スキャン、デジタル化等の無断複製は著作権法上での例外を除き禁じられています。本書を代行業者等の第三者に依頼してスキャンやデジタル化することは、たとえ個人や家庭内での利用であっても著作権法上認められておりません。